IMAGES OF
LOST LONDON

IMAGES OF
LOST LONDON
1875-1945

PHILIP DAVIES

ATLANTIC PUBLISHING

Acknowledgements

This publication is an abridged edition of *Lost London 1870-1945* first published in 2009.

With the exception of those listed below, all the photographs in this publication were taken from the collection of the former Greater London Council Historic Buildings Division. Upon the abolition of the GLC in 1984 the print collection was transferred to the London Region of English Heritage where it remains in daily use for reference purposes. The negatives are held by the London Metropolitan Archives. The illustrations in this book are protected by copyright and may only be reproduced by permission of English Heritage or the London Metropolitan Archives, or other third party copyright owner, depending on the source of the image.

National Monuments Record: p10 Westminster Embankment; p108 Shad Thames; p110 Pool of London
Guildhall Library: p1 Oxford Arms; p25 Sir Paul Pindar's House
Tower Hamlets Local Library and Archives: p9 Cats' Meat Man; p98 East India Dock Road

Published by Atlantic Publishing 2012
Atlantic Publishing, 38 Copthorne Road, Croxley Green, Hertfordshire, WD3 4AQ

ISBN: 978-1-909242-04-3
Printed and bound in the UK

CONTENTS

INTRODUCTION

London was the first great metropolis of the industrial age. In 1800 it was a major European city of one million inhabitants. By 1911 it was the greatest city in the world – the first city of the British Empire with over seven million people – greater than the combined populations of Paris, Berlin, St Petersburg and Moscow. This phenomenal expansion was unique in Europe – both for the speed of its growth and the way in which it happened. Even today London remains unlike any other European city with its own distinctive form which is a direct result of its history.

London was never controlled by a single political or religious body able to guide the layout of its streets to one grand design. It was the largely-unplanned creation of a pluralist society driven by trade and commercial imperatives. In the aftermath of the Great Fire of 1666, the evanescent visions of Christopher Wren, Robert Hooke and John Evelyn evaporated like morning mist before the rising sun of commercial resurgence. London always was, and still remains, a city founded on commerce, flourishing today as a world centre for the trading of financial services.

London's expansion in the 18th and 19th centuries was driven by speculative development. Pragmatic contracts between wealthy landowners and opportunistic builders were regulated by the leasehold system; the former in search of long-term income, and the latter by the prospect of turning a quick profit.

Narrow timber-framed houses were the established building type in London before the Great Fire. The average twelve feet plot width was dictated by the maximum length of structural timber. A significant number of these houses survived the Fire well into the 20th century on the fringes of the City of London in Smithfield, Holborn, Aldgate and Borough, providing a very tangible link with the mediaeval past. Their distinctive gables and jettied upper storeys can be seen in the photographs, often heavily overlain by subsequent alterations. On the expiry of leases, it was quite common for such houses to be encased in brick, or given a polite facade, rather than completely redeveloped; many London houses, whilst ostensibly similar, embraced much older structures and interiors beneath – individual metaphors for the city as a whole.

In the wake of the Great Fire, various London Building Acts were passed – in 1667, 1707 and 1709 – specifying common standards of construction. Increasingly, brick replaced timber for external use which facilitated much greater external uniformity. The earliest surviving example of a row of matching London town houses can be found at Nos 52-55 Newington Green. Built in 1658, they pre-date the Fire, but in the reconstruction of London after 1666, the brick terrace became the established urban form, creating a key component of what made London unique as a European city.

Nicholas Barbon (d1698), a financier, builder and adventurer, refined the system of speculative leasehold development through which much of Georgian and Victorian London was built. Various builders undertook to construct small numbers of houses within a particular development, often overseen by the landowner or his agent. In order to ensure consistency, the row of uniformly-designed houses evolved and became fashionable. This form of housing was remarkably versatile, providing flexible accommodation for a whole variety of uses – houses, taverns, offices, shops and workshops – usually with a private rear yard, or garden. Short rows of terraced housing were built in central and inner London, but also as ribbon development in outlying areas along the main roads such as Mile End, Chiswick, Tottenham and Peckham.

Often minor variations in window heights or parapet levels marked the work of each builder, but the overall aspiration was greater uniformity. In the first half of the 18th century this trend towards understated regularity was reinforced by the Palladian revival. Carved doorcases and other elaborate sculptural enrichment were eschewed in favour of external sobriety and abstract qualities of proportion.

In 1774, the Building Acts were consolidated into a new London Building Act which specified different 'rates' of houses. This dictated the form and design of much of London for over a century and created the city which can be seen in these photographs. The floor area set the rate, which in turn determined the thickness of the principal walls. Like industrial products, a family of building types emerged – from the highest first rate house with a five bay frontage and a linked mews building to the modest fifth rate dwelling just one room deep.

Much of Georgian and early Victorian London owes its remarkable unity to the increasingly standardised approach to

elevations drawn up by estate surveyors. This is why 18th and 19th century housing looks so similar in areas as diverse as Camberwell, Bloomsbury and Bow. The serial construction of whole neighbourhoods of planned streets and squares on the private landed estates of central and inner London was a process of continuous refinement, and it created a distinctive city completely unlike anything else in Europe. "While the Continental architect considered it his task to make the fronts of the building as imaginative as possible, the English endeavoured to let them express what had to be said in the simplest and most concise way". Nevertheless, these plain, understated exteriors often concealed lavish interiors with elaborate ornamental plasterwork and joinery.

One of the unique characteristics of this city was, and still remains, the London square. Terraces of individual houses, each subordinated to the wider composition, were set around a communal garden area enclosed by railings for the private enjoyment of surrounding residents. By 1900 there were over 460 across the capital. As well as providing much needed oases

Piccadilly Circus, 1893: the symbolic centre of the British Empire: Alfred Gilbert's Angel of Christian Charity, was unveiled in 1893 as a memorial to the 7th Earl of Shaftesbury, the great philanthropist and social reformer. It rapidly became the haunt of flower-sellers, newspaper boys and London's louche nightlife.

of green space, they created a highly distinctive urban grain which imparted a unity to the city as a whole and linked the wealthiest with the poorest districts.

But there was another much more subtle reason for the remarkable cohesion of Georgian and early Victorian London, long since forgotten; a secret ingredient which conferred an innate harmony on the city, and which influenced everything from the layout of an entire neighbourhood to the size of a window pane – the Imperial system of measures.

Neighbourhoods were laid out by surveyors who used acres, furlongs, rods and chains – measurements which had been in common usage for marking out arable land since the 9th century. An acre was the length of a furlong (or furrow's

Regent Street c 1906: The reconstruction of Nash's Regent Street was one of the greatest redevelopments ever seen in London. Nos. 17-25 Regent Street, depicted here at the junction with Jermyn Street, boasted unusual Ammonite capitals.

length), 660ft, and its width was one chain, 66ft. For shorter lengths a perch, a pole or a rod were used. There were four rods to one chain. A London workman's house had a frontage of one rod or 16ft 6inches. In East London, one chain corresponded to four house frontages, so entire districts were created based on endogenous proportional relationships. The builders used rules divided into feet and inches, or fathoms (the length of outstretched arms), which meant that the actual proportions deployed for the construction of public spaces, houses and their internal furnishings were derived directly from the human form, which accounts for their inherent unity. Covent Garden, for instance, was laid out as 6 x 5 chains and Belgrave Square as 10 x 10 chains, or 10 acres.

Thus the late Georgian/early Victorian city was infused by a common system of harmonious proportions, from the layout of an entire area to the pattern of its paving. Much of the subsequent development of London saw the fragmentation of this unified whole – with the coming of the railways, road

widening, metropolitan improvements and the construction of larger buildings on aggregated plots for a whole variety of new uses. Nevertheless, a great deal of this urban backcloth still remains in areas like Islington, Bloomsbury, Hackney, Camberwell and Lambeth.

As London expanded relentlessly outwards from its bi-polar centres in the City of London and Westminster, it embraced and later subsumed older village cores and outlying areas, many of which retained rural and vernacular buildings, normally associated with a rural idyll, surviving well into the 20th century; Rotherhithe, with its weatherboarded cottages, had a greater affinity with the fishing villages of the Thames Estuary than the great maw of London.

Timber remained common for smaller Georgian houses until well into the mid-18th century, particularly near the river where there was a ready supply of timber from the wharves and warehouses serving the Baltic and North American trade. Sometimes this was concealed behind brick facades, but often houses were fully weatherboarded. Rare today, many survived into the 20th century, as can be discerned in the photographs of Bermondsey, Rotherhithe, Lambeth and Limehouse. In these outlying areas, there was a creative intermingling of the urban tradition of 'polite' architecture with long-established rural vernacular traditions, which reached into town from the east along the river and from the surrounding Home Counties.

In the poorer areas, away from estate control, development pressures were intense as speculative builders vied to cram as many fifth rate dwellings into as small a space as possible. The result was the sort of housing which can be seen at Bankside and across many parts of the East End with families densely packed into tight networks of sunless courts and blind alleys, sharing communal privies, with a single tap or pump providing (frequently contaminated) water for an entire parish. A handful of the more fortunate lived in charitable almshouses erected by City livery companies, or local parishes for the deserving poor.

In the mid-19th century urban life was a nightmare for the poorer classes. Until the "Sanitary Idea" promoted by reformers such as Edwin Chadwick and Southwood Smith began to make headway in the 1850s, the concept of environmental health was as alien to Victorian minds as the connection between dirt and disease. Cholera was thought to be a miasmatic vapour transmitted by foul air. Dustheaps and middens the size of four-storey houses attracted scavengers or 'bunters' who made a living from reclaiming anything of value. The largest, a huge dustheap at King's Cross, was the setting for Noddy Boffin's business in Dickens' Our Mutual Friend.

By 1900, after 50 years of metropolitan improvements and sanitary reform, some of the worst nuisances of the previous decades had been addressed, but poverty was still endemic and life expectancy much lower for the indigent poor. In 1850 in London the average life expectancy at birth was 38 compared with the national average of 41. By 1890 it had risen to 44 compared with 46 nationally, but these figures concealed terrible differentials. In 1900 a person in the West End had twice the life expectancy of a person in the East End. The average age at death in the West End was 55. In the East End it was 30.

Childhood mortality rates were even more shocking. In the West End 18% of children died before the age of 5; in the East End 55%. In some streets, Jack London noted "out of every hundred children born in a year, fifty-five die before they are five years old".

The construction of new bridges in the early 19th century opened up new areas south of the river for development beyond the ancient centres of Borough and Lambeth. Here was London's service area lined with a chaotic jumble of wharves, warehouses and noxious industries; dark canyons separated by slit-like alleys leading to river stairs and jetties. Many, such as those in Shad Thames, Bermondsey and Rotherhithe, still survive, converted into stylish loft apartments, demonstrating the innate versatility and sustainability of so much of London's historic fabric. Particular areas were distinguished by their smells. Bermondsey, for instance, was rank with the smell of leather tanning, breweries and vinegar vats.

For many, the corner pub provided transient solace. In 1905 gin sold at 41/2d a quarter and beer at 1d for a half-pint. In poorer areas some pubs were little more than domestic buildings given over to the sale of alcohol but others, were glittering palaces of cut-glass and polychromatic tiles, their seductive pleasures announced in the refulgent glow from myriad massive gas lanterns: beacons of light in a world of bleak horizons.

But for all the social deprivation, poverty and underprivilege, comments on East End life were all too often coloured by the superficial perception of outsiders. For those who actually lived in the poorer districts of London, stoical cheerfulness was the most commonly recognised quality epitomised by the Cockney with a ready wit and readiness to laugh.

In 1900 London was an extraordinary kaleidoscope of districts with a constantly shifting social geography as areas declined, prospered or were redeveloped with bewildering rapidity.

The cats' meat man, c 1902.
Once a familiar sight in the poorer districts of London, many a poor wife resorted to discarded meat or offal to feed her unsuspecting family. The house in the background is emblazoned with ER to celebrate the coronation of Edward VII.

Imperial London: Westminster Embankment c 1895 with the newly-completed National Liberal Club to the right, Whitehall Court beyond and a cabmen's shelter with a line of hansoms in the foreground. The great departments of state were being transformed with palatial new offices which expressed the political and commercial might of the British Empire.

There is no doubt at all that the growth of the early conservation movement was driven by a reaction against the massive scale of the changes that were transforming late 19th century London into a great imperial and commercial capital and at the wholesale destruction of old buildings that accompanied it. Successive waves of railway construction from 1836 onwards, compounded later by the underground railway, cut huge swathes through the metropolis. Increasingly, the repetitive terraces of the 18th and 19th century city, that had once imparted such a remarkable unity to the capital, were being scythed through by massive waves of reconstruction.

With the relentless expansion of London's population, major metropolitan improvements cut further swathes through some of London's most historic neighbourhoods. In the City of London, Cannon Street had been widened as early as the 1850s, but later improvements were even more radical. In the 1860s a whole series of new thoroughfares were driven through the Cities of London and Westminster. Queen Victoria Street

radically altered the geometry and grain of the City of London, whilst in the 1860s the creation of Holborn Viaduct and Farringdon Street transformed the entire morphology of the area between the City of London and the poorer districts to the west around Hatton Garden, triggered by the colossal metropolitan market improvements at Smithfield, one of the greatest exercises of Victorian civic improvement ever seen in Britain – a massive, multi-layered complex of grand new market buildings designed by the City Surveyor, Sir Horace Jones, superimposed over a network of subterranean railways.

The momentum of civic improvement continued remorselessly. Proposals for a major new road between Holborn and the Strand had been discussed for over 60 years before they came to fruition in 1905. They entailed the comprehensive redevelopment of a huge area, the eviction of over 3,700 people and the eradication of one of London's worst slums around Drury Lane and Clare Market. These were photographed systematically as the entire neighbourhood was reconfigured for the formation of the great new commercial boulevards of Kingsway and Aldwych, which over the next twenty years were lined with majestic classical buildings reflecting the commercial might of the British Empire. In the process, some of inner London's most historic areas were destroyed completely. Among the most grievous losses was the clearance of Holywell Street and Wych Street, regarded as the most picturesque in

London, and which contained one of the finest concentrations of pre-Fire houses in the capital. Today, only the erroneously named Old Curiosity Shop, No. 13 Portsmouth Street and a sole survivor – the White Horse public house in Clements Inn Passage – predate the Edwardian improvements.

In the City and West End, large swathes of central London were reconstructed in grand Edwardian Beaux Arts style in a magnificent expression of civic pride and commercial and imperial self-confidence. In the City vast new citadels were raised for commerce, banking and insurance. The massive, forbidding hulk of Newgate Prison was demolished for the spectacular new Central Criminal Courts in 1903. Even the old Christ's Hospital, a City institution for over 300 years, succumbed when it was relocated to Horsham and its site redeveloped.

As the pace of change quickened, the preservation of historic buildings began to be seen as a popular cause for the educated middle-classes, and as an integral part of the emerging interest in town planning and philanthropy. In 1879 William Morris founded the Society for the Protection of Ancient Buildings (SPAB) "to keep watch on old monuments" and "to protect against all 'restoration' that means more than keeping out wind and weather".

In 1889 The London Topographical Society was formed. In 1893-95 Octavia Hill, Robert Hunter and Canon Hardwicke Rawnsley, a keen amateur photographer, founded the National Trust for Places of Historic Interest and Natural Beauty, which drew together interest in protecting landscapes with enthusiasm for preserving historic buildings. It attracted 250 members in its first year. Initially the Trust worked with private companies to help keep historic buildings in use. The restoration of Staple Inn by the Prudential Assurance Company under the watchful eye of the SPAB was an early success.

Growing public unease at both the scale and pace of change was expressed both in the press and in parliamentary committees, but in 1893 the demolition of the finest building in East London – the old Royal Palace at Bromley-by-Bow for a London County Council (LCC) Board School provoked widespread comment. In exasperation at the unthinking and unplanned destruction of so much of London's architectural heritage, a group of private individuals came together to form the London Survey Committee with the primary aim of recording buildings before they were destroyed.

Charing Cross, 1932. Seen here surrounded by cars, a replica of the original mediaeval Eleanor Cross, designed by E M Barry with sculpture by Thomas Earp, was erected on the forecourt of Charing Cross station in 1863. The original, which stood at the end of Whitehall, was pulled down in 1647, and the site later occupied by Le Sueur's famous equestrian statue of Charles I.

The work of the London Survey Committee was hugely important for the growth of the conservation movement. Increasingly, preservation was identified with progressive planning and utilitarian ideals rather than just whimsical antiquarianism. The preservation of historic buildings, parks and open spaces was seen as an integral part of a wider social idealism – the provision of the proper amenities of life for a great city and for adequate housing for the poor; a concept taken up and given substance in the Utopian visions which underpinned the new Garden Suburbs, which were being built on the fringes of London at Brentham, Hampstead, Ealing and elsewhere.

The Survey Committee soon worked in close partnership with the LCC. Subsequently it was absorbed into the LCC, and much later it became the Greater London Council (GLC) Historic Buildings Committee. With the abolition of the GLC in 1984, the old GLC Historic Buildings Division and its Historic Buildings Committee were united with the newly-formed English Heritage. The London Advisory Committee of English Heritage continues this valuable role today. Over 100 years since its creation, it still provides advice on all major development affecting London's historic environment.

From 1900 to 1914 London underwent a public transport revolution that facilitated the development of outlying areas into new residential suburbs. The electrification of the railways and tramways, and the development of the deep tube and bus network precipitated major population shifts. In the 10 years from 1901 over 55,000 people, 12% of the population,

migrated from inner London, most to the new suburbs. Journeys on public transport virtually doubled over the same period from 142 to 250 per head of population.

With the outbreak of the First World War, shortages of both labour and supplies torpedoed many of London's Edwardian "grands projets". The reconstruction of Regent Street, Kingsway and County Hall ground to a halt, together with most new house building when, in 1916, all new building was proscribed under the Defence of the Realm Act.

In the period following the First World War, rising land values, population growth and the demands of the car generated intense commercial pressures for new development and further waves of metropolitan improvements. The pre-war momentum for new buildings for a new age re-emerged with even greater vigour as department stores, cinemas, commercial buildings, government offices and blocks of flats transformed the face of the capital.

By 1927 the population of London had reached 7,800,000, an increase of 20% in just 25 years fuelled by the expansion of the public transport network. The first bus stops arrived in the 1920s and buses with roofs were introduced in 1925. The extension of a sophisticated network of buses and electric tramways facilitated the development of new outlying areas like East Sheen, Wimbledon, Kingston and Teddington, whilst the radical expansion of the underground and surface railways generated unprecedented opportunities for further suburban growth. In 1921, Dagenham, for example, was a struggling parish on the eastern fringe of London with a population of less than 10,000. In six years it had grown into a town of 50,000 with 'homes fit for heroes' to live in.

In the inter-war years the height, massing and bulk of central London underwent a step-change. Many were apoplectic at the changes. Having celebrated London as The Unique City, the Dane, Steen Eiler Rasmussen, castigated the introduction of continental experiments and ideas, which he believed were unsuited to London's character, particularly the replacement of conventional London streets with large estates of flats for public housing. Inter-war residential development was shaped by powerful centrifugal forces. Between 1921 and 1938 almost 200,000 people were displaced from central and inner London by slum clearance projects and Council housing programmes. Most never returned to their old neighbourhoods where large blocks of Council flats replaced the terraced houses, yards and alleys of Victorian London, dispersing many old communities in a Cockney diaspora. Waves of successive migration pushed people out from the centre into the inner ring, which, in turn, eroded the cohesion of middle-class communities, who moved out to the suburbs.

By 1939 the population of Greater London was 8.2 million – well ahead of New York with 6.93 million. It was not just the largest city in the world, it was its largest port, handling twice the tonnage of Liverpool. It was the seat of government, the monarchy and the judiciary. It was the cosmopolitan capital of the British Empire at the moment of its greatest extent. It financed half the world's trade, while the volume of its manufacturing output exceeded that of any of the great industrial conurbations of the Midlands and the North. It was the focal point of the road and rail network; the primary cultural centre with many of the leading museums and galleries of the age containing world-famous collections. London was the pre-eminent world city, the dynamo that powered Britain and widely acknowledged to be the finest city in the world. But with one-fifth of Britain's population concentrated into just 610 sq miles, by 1939 London was also a shockingly vulnerable target.

Today it is difficult to comprehend the scale of wartime destruction. In one night alone, on Sunday, 29 December 1940, the City of London lost about a third of its entire floorspace. The ensuing fire, which could be seen 30 miles away, leapt the river and ignited a line of warehouses on the south bank between London Bridge and Tower Bridge. Almost every building between Moorgate and Aldersgate Street was obliterated, including the ancient maze of streets and alleys around Paternoster Row in the shadow of St Paul's. Over 6

Featherstone Buildings, Holborn, 9 May 1941
Holborn suffered the highest per capita casualty rate from bombing in London.

million books burned in the flames. Tragically, old buildings were the most vulnerable. While modern steel-framed buildings withstood high explosives and fire relatively well, older masonry structures simply collapsed.

By the end of the war the level of damage was truly shocking, 50,000 houses destroyed or irreparable in inner London alone, and over 60,000 in outer London. An additional 290,000 houses suffered serious damage and a further 2 million or more slight damage.

A whole series of factors determined the form and pattern of post-war reconstruction – not least radical idealism coupled with an unprecedented opportunity to create a socially-engineered New Jerusalem. With the exception of major landmark buildings, in the headlong rush to embrace the future there was little appetite for retaining the past. Whole streets of perfectly serviceable, but damaged, houses were left to rot by speculative developers, or abandoned by local authorities determined to build a fairer and more socially just society. In many parts of inner London and the East End the opportunity was seized to clear large areas of insanitary and sub-standard housing in a concerted effort to improve social conditions. As a result even greater damage was inflicted on historic areas which had survived the Luftwaffe, through comprehensive redevelopment, particularly in the poorer areas of inner and east London – at King Square, Finsbury, for instance, or Bromley-by-Bow, which was virtually wiped off the map by an unholy alliance of comprehensive redevelopment and massive new highway engineering.

However, there were some who stood against the tide of comprehensive redevelopment in favour of a more delicate form of urban surgery and place-making. Many of the great architectural set-pieces such as Buckingham Palace and the Palace of Westminster were repaired with painstaking authenticity. The landed estates of the West End which exercised freehold control – the Crown, Grosvenor, Portman, Bedford and Howard de Walden, for instance, took a much longer and more enlightened view of their stewardship. By and large they carefully stitched back the damaged fabric of their buildings and streets to their pre-war appearance.

Today it is possible to walk from the Embankment through Inner and Middle Temple, past Street's magnificent Law Courts, through Lincoln's Inn, across High Holborn to Gray's Inn and beyond into Bloomsbury and still appreciate their historic qualities The primary reason for this was the unfashionable approach adopted by the privately-owned Inns in insisting upon recreating the qualities which made a place special – based on a deep understanding that the importance of the place transcended the sum of its component parts. This was achieved in the face of intense opposition by local

St Andrew-by-the-Wardrobe, 29 February 1941
The devastation of war: the burnt-out interior showing sheet lead hanging from the aisle roofs. Just under half of the City's churches were damaged or destroyed by wartime bombing.

authorities, and of scorn from the modernist architectural establishment of the day, who strongly favoured sweeping the past away for comprehensive redevelopment. Yet with the benefit of hindsight who was more progressive in their approach to placemaking?

Britain now leads the world in the sophistication of its mechanisms for managing change to its historic environment. One of the reasons London has become so successful is that public pressure has brought about a much better balance between continuity and change which, in turn, has enhanced the capital's appeal to overseas investors and visitors. Londoners care passionately about the places where they live as much as individual buildings. Increasingly, historic buildings are seen as an asset, not a constraint on progress. They command a premium in the open market, and, at a time when it is imperative to reduce carbon emissions, it is recognised that the creative reuse of old buildings is inherently sustainable, reutilising the embodied energy they contain. Routinely, warehouses, tenements, factories and other old buildings are being adapted, converted and reused by developers who have realised, at last, that history sells and a better way to build the New Jerusalem lies in the imaginative recycling of those 'dark satanic mills'.

Above: Shepherd's Place Archway and Tenter Street, Spitalfields, 10 May 1909

Shepherd's Place archway (1810) with Tenter Street beyond. The houses on the old Tenter Ground estate were mean and closely-packed with little space at the rear. Chronic poverty was endemic, the main access to the estate was through this single archway from White's Row. What happened to these people?

Chapter One

THE CITY FRINGE

The loosely-defined arc of inner London from Clerkenwell and Smithfield in the north-west to Spitalfields and Minories in the south-east is referred to commonly as the City Fringe.

Clustered around St John's Gate and the old Priory Church of St John of Jerusalem, Clerkenwell is depicted on the cusp of change as ancient streets of 17th and 18th century domestic buildings were giving way to new light industrial and commercial premises. At a time when scant regard was given to architectural conservation, the preservation of St John's Church is an indication of the growing awareness of the importance of retaining London's architectural treasures.

To the south, Smithfield, or Smoothfield, was a large expanse of marshy land on the edge of the City used for mediaeval tournaments and, before Tyburn, as a place of execution. It was here in 1305 that Sir William Wallace was hanged, drawn and quartered, and where in 1557 the Protestant martyrs were burned under the Marian persecution. The famous cattle market was established in 1638, but in 1855 the sale and slaughter of live animals moved to Caledonian Market. A huge new meat market served by underground railways was erected to the designs of the City Surveyor, Sir Horace Jones.

Cloth Fair takes its name from an important cloth market, St Bartholomew's Fair, its tolls supporting the adjacent Priory and hospital. Held for three days from the eve of St Bartholomew on 24 August, it was opened by the Lord Mayor cutting a piece of cloth – the origin of the cutting of a ribbon to open buildings or events. The Fair had its own court – the Court of Pie Powder – which had jurisdiction over commercial complaints, weights and measures, and theft. It was notorious for immorality, crime and public disorder. "Knavery is here in perfection, dextrous cutpurses and pickpockets", wrote a French visitor in 1698. In a concerted effort to clean up the area it was abolished when the cattle market moved in 1855. The eponymous Cloth Fair can be seen here – a remarkable series of mediaeval, timber-framed houses which survived well into the 20th century, many of which were still in use by dealers in second-hand clothes and rags.

Further east the great merchant houses of Georgian Spitalfields are portrayed clinging to vestiges of their original elegance, even though by 1900 many had fallen into multiple occupation as cheap lodging houses. Hit by cheap French imports, silk weaving had virtually collapsed by 1860 generating massive hardship and an economic vacuum filled by mass immigration from Eastern Europe. By 1900 only a handful of weavers remained in Bethnal Green.

A working neighbourhood

Above left: Bishops Court, Aylesbury Street, Clerkenwell, 28 October 1904

A typical inner city courtyard development built in 1726-28, and probably always intended for multiple occupation. The chimney in the background carries a sign for John Smith & Son, Steam Clock Factory. Smith's manufactured the clock tower which still stands at the junction of City Road and Goswell Road.

Above right: The Old Dick Whittington Inn, Cloth Fair, 16 May 1904

"It was pleasant … to sit through winter's amethystine dusk and watch the fire and its play of shadows … sportive, fantastic shadows, which hovered and darted, and sometimes made a long arm as if to snatch the very tankard out of one's hand."

(R Thurston Hopkins 1927)

Allegedly the oldest inn in London, the Old Dick Whittington was demolished in 1916. Two carved wooden satyrs of 1550 from its corner posts are in the Museum of London.

Right: 11 St John's Square, 30 January 1907

In this oblique view the earlier 17th century building can be seen clearly behind the skin of the later front facade. The posters are of particular interest. The *Weekly Dispatch* leads with the "The Great Tichborne Mystery" and *Lloyds News* with "The Jamaica Earthquake" for its Sunday edition on 20 January.

Opposite: Cloth Fair, Smithfield, 27 July 1908

A fine group of 17th century timber-framed houses between the north door of St Bartholomew's Church and West Smithfield prior to demolition.

EVANS & WITT
STATIONERS & BOOKBINDERS.

BOOKSELLERS & TOBACCONISTS.

71A ☞ **C. BURRELL,** ☞ **71A**
DEALER in PICKLED TONGUES, SWEETBREADS &c

SMOKE **WILL'S's**
"OLD FLAKE" CIGARETTES.

CHEAP STATIONERY STORES.

PRIORY CHURCH
S. BARTHOLOMEW
The GREAT

BRANDAUERS
PENS

EVANS & WITT

BOILED BEEF

Narrow lanes of crooked, overhanging houses...

Opposite: Gatehouse to the Church of St Bartholomew the Great, Smithfield, 18 November 1908
St Bartholomew the Great, built by Rahere in 1123, is London's oldest parish church. This polite Georgian facade was destroyed in a Zeppelin raid in 1916 revealing the original 16th century timber-framed frontage behind. It was restored in the 1920s.

Above left: Rear elevation of the gatehouse to St Bartholomew the Great, 18 November 1908
The entrance passage to the church.

Left: Cloth Fair, Smithfield, 16 May 1904
"Here are narrow walled lanes, where two persons can pass one another with difficulty … The explorer may thread covered passages from which he can note details of domestic life passing within easy ken. That houses built so closely, and of such inflammable material, should have survived to the present day seems little short of marvellous." (William Dixon)
The view from Schoolden Street depicting a small 17th century dwelling against the walls of St Bartholomew's church.

Above right: Cockerills Buildings, Red Lion Passage, Cloth Fair, 26 March 1912
View looking east. The buttress of St Bartholomew's Church can be glimpsed in the middle distance.

Worn by time

Above: 20 Cloth Fair and entrance to Red Lion Passage looking west, 26 March 1912
Note the patriotic paper lanterns for sale in the shop window and the sign for the Fat and Bone merchant on the extreme right. The newspaper placard features French Motor Bandits. Three Killed. Wooden scaffolding was common at this time.

Left: Bartholomew Close, 1906
Weatherboarded timber-framed house with a grocer's shop on the ground floor. The arrival of the photographer was an occasion of considerable local curiosity. Hats were a mark of respectability; note the variety of headgear – top hats, bowlers and cloth caps are worn by men and boys of all ages.

Left: 51-54 Bartholomew Close, Smithfield, 7 October 1909
The premises of S Crouch & Son, Shop and Office Fitters, general builders and signwriters. No. 51 is occupied by J Potter, a dealer in second-hand cloth and paper, a trade once common in the area. The front wall with the cart behind retains its original wooden posts and railings. The original thick-section glazing bars to the windows are typical early 18th century details.

Above: 78-80 Bartholomew Close, 7 October 1909
View looking north towards the entrance to St Bartholomew's Church with early 18th century houses to the right.

Above: 39-40 Norton Folgate, Spitalfields, 25 March 1909

Norton Folgate at Bishopsgate Street Without – the boundary between Shoreditch and the City of London. The elaborate stone boundary plaque is dated 1846. The photographic studio on the extreme left offers coloured or enamelled miniatures for 1/-. The hairdressers is the home of the Norton Folgate Toilet Club. p24 shows the wider view immediately to the south.

Ancient city boundary

Above: Norton Folgate Court House, Folgate Street, 6 October 1909

This late 17th century building became the court house for the manor and liberty of Norton Folgate in 1744. An upper room was used for the court house, and a lower room as a watch house until the abolition of the liberty and its incorporation into the Borough of Stepney in 1900. On the extreme left, beside the corner shop and downpipes, is a fragment of mediaeval stonework alleged to be the remains of St Mary Spital Priory.

Right: 10-11 Norton Folgate, 25 March 1909

The Golden Eagle was a dispensing chemist founded in 1750 with a delightful double-bowed shop front of about 1780, a railed stall board and brass cill bands engraved with the names of the store – Peter Jones. The traditional apothecaries' jars can be seen in the left-hand window. No. 10 was occupied continuously by lead and glass merchants from 1809 until the 20th century.

By the Bishop's Gate

Above: Bishopsgate Street Without looking south from boundary with Norton Folgate, October 1909
Even on the edge of the City of London, the original mediaeval house plots persist filled by 18th and 19th century buildings of a domestic scale and character. Such areas of the City fringe serviced the daily needs of the great temples of commerce further south in the heart of the City.

Left: Bishopsgate Street (west side) looking north to Norton Folgate, 7 October 1909
A typical street scene on the City fringe at the beginning of the 20th century. The shops boast elaborate gas lanterns and signs; street orderly bins of the type shown in the foreground are still in widespread use in the City of London.

Opposite: View of Sir Paul Pindar's house, Bishopsgate, c 1885.
The dismantling and re-erection of the famous frontage of this 16th century merchant's house was an indication of growing antiquarian interest in London's vanishing past.

Faded grandeur

Opposite above: Spital Square looking towards No.22 with St Mary's Passage beyond, 3 May 1909
Nos. 5-9 Spital Square (left) were built as a terrace c 1704. Nos. 5 and 6 were remodelled during the Regency with faux stone-coursed stucco, wrought iron balustrades and an elaborate iron lamp overthrow to No.5. Beyond is the German Synagogue (1858) in a heavy classical style. The cleanliness of the street, the absence of clutter and the innate sense of visual order are particularly notable.

Above: St Mary's Passage and Lamb Street from Spital Square, October 1909
No. 1 St Mary's Passage was a large, double-fronted merchant's house built in 1733 by Samuel Worrall, a local carpenter. Giant Doric pilasters frame the frontage. By the mid-19th century it had become a police station, although by the time of this photograph it was in use as a workshop and lodging house.

Opposite below: St Katherine's Dock House, Tower, c 1910
Superb cast iron ornamental lamp standards on the forecourt of St Katherine's Dock House, which was destroyed in the Blitz in 1940. The former Royal Mint building, designed by James Johnson and built by Sir Robert Smirke 1807-12, can be seen clearly to the right. In the middle distance is the GNR Goods Depot. Note the complete absence of road traffic.

Corner of Jewry Street & Aldgate, c 1906
This superb group of 17th century timber-framed houses stood at the
junction of Jewry Street and Aldgate. Photographed for their antiquarian
interest by the London Stereoscopic and Photographic Society, the images
were annotated by hand with the names of the premises. The lath and plaster
finishes and timber studwork are exposed clearly on the corner house.

Chapter Two

THE CITY

The City of London is shown on the cusp of change. The old Roman and mediaeval grain of the City is still very apparent in the maze of narrow lanes and alleys, whilst groups of domestic buildings of all periods conferred a great sense of history until the Second World War. Numerous old, timber pre-Fire houses could be found on the edges of the City around Aldgate, Fleet Street and Cloth Fair, and many streets were still punctuated by later, brick, Georgian town houses, once occupied by City merchants, but later converted to commercial use or offices.

In 1851 the resident population of the City had been 129,000, many of whom were shopkeepers, tailors, craftsmen and artisans. A large amount of manufacturing still took place over the shop and in small factories and workshops, but by 1901 the population had shrunk to just 27,000. Many small traders and craftsmen migrated to the City fringe, or to new, purpose-built commercial premises. Increasingly the characteristic domestic scale and form of the City underwent a step change. By 1905 four-fifths of the entire City had been rebuilt in the previous 50 years, doubling the amount of available floorspace for the banks, insurance companies, shipping agents and brokers that financed half the world's trade. Entire street blocks were felled for gigantic new temples of commerce as older residential buildings gave way to monumental palaces which overtly expressed British commercial pre-eminence. The City's residential population was replaced by armies of office workers, who commuted daily via the great railway termini and on the underground and, later, the deep tube.

Whilst the livery halls of the wealthy City guilds held their own and prospered alongside dozens of pre-Fire and Wren churches, other great City institutions succumbed. Christ's Hospital moved out in 1902 hard on the heels of Charterhouse School, which had relocated to Godalming in 1874. Newgate Prison was cleared in the same year to make way for the Central Criminal Courts, and Smirke's elegant General Post Office was rendered redundant by a huge new Post Office on the site of Christ's Hospital.

Hidden antiquity

Above: 47-52 Aldgate High Street, 27 September 1908
Christopher Hill's wine shop is now the Hoop and Grapes public house, which has 13th century cellars and a listening tube to the bars overhead to allow the landlord to eavesdrop on conversations. Two ancient carved oak posts flank the entrance. It is one of the oldest taverns in London.

Middle right: 4-7 Aldgate, 30 August 1909
The Metropole Restaurant occupied part of the old Saracens Head Inn, a fine 17th century coaching inn with timber-framing overlain with elaborate carved Corinthian pilasters, which on demolition were salvaged by the Guildhall Museum. Note the Select Ladies Dining Room on the first floor at no extra charge. Behind the timber balustraded parapet is a roof terrace with a recessed weatherboarded garret and clay tile roof. Harris's Restaurant clearly catered for a different clientele. Beside the bunches of bananas in the window of Levy's shop is the entrance to Saracens Head Yard.

Below right: St Botolph Aldgate Charity School, c 1907
The Charity School, built in 1793, was demolished for the Tower Bridge Approach road improvements. The gate lodge to the Royal Mint can be seen to the right. Note the superb street surfaces with randomly-laid cobbles in the foreground, the setted carriageway and York stone footway beyond.

Opposite: 7 Jewry Street, Aldgate, 20 August 1909
No. 7 Jewry Street was built in 1650. It survived both the Great Fire and the Blitz, which destroyed the buildings on either side, before succumbing to a fire in 1946. The old clay tile roof can be seen behind the Victorian gable. J E Sly & Son, a well-known firm of rope, sack and bag manufacturers, occupied the house from the early 19th century. The figure in the first floor window is probably one of the Sly family.

Vanished Minories

Above: Holy Trinity Minories, 14 October 1913
The Abbey of Graces of the Blessed Virgin was founded in 1293 for Minorite or Franciscan nuns. After the Dissolution, it was adapted for use as a parish church and later rebuilt in a severe Georgian style in 1706. The church was destroyed by enemy action in 1940.

Right: Three Crown Court, Minories, 14 October 1913
Typical alley and courtyard; a mediaeval form which once characterised much of the City of London and its fringes.

The cusp of change

The erection of a palatial new headquarters for the Port of London Authority to the designs of Sir Edwin Cooper necessitated the clearance of a huge block of Georgian properties to the north and east of Trinity Square. This was typical of much of the development in the City of London at this time as older domestic-scaled buildings gave way to sumptuous new monumental buildings.

Above: Savage Gardens, Tower, 20 June 1913
View looking north from Trinity Square with the side of Trinity House to the right.

Right: Catherine Court, 25 January 1913
Catherine Court was a narrow court of early Georgian houses between Seething Lane and Trinity Square enclosed at each end by wrought iron gates. The plaque is dated 1725. The poster on the wall advertises the sale of antique fixtures and fittings from the houses. The fine carved Corinthian porch to the double-fronted house on the right was sold for £145, the equivalent of £7,500 today.

Trading the wealth of grain

Above left: Corn Exchange, Mark Lane, c 1908
The Corn Exchange was erected in 1828 with a handsome arcade of fluted Greek Doric columns to the front surmounted by the royal arms. Factors, farmers, seedgrowers and millers gathered here to trade in grain. However, with the arrival of the motor car, and the disappearance of the horse from London, trade declined. By 1928 it was losing £90,000 per annum. It was demolished three years later.

Above right: 33-35 Mark Lane, 7 March 1910
A superb staircase of c 1710 with richly carved balusters of varying patterns. The twisted corner newel post boasts an intricately carved base and Corinthian capital.

Below left: 33-35 Mark Lane, 7 March 1910
The entrance hall: beautifully carved entrance screen and cornice. Part of a lead statue, which once stood in the garden, can be seen behind the door.

Opposite above: Crutched Friars, 20 June 1912
View along Crutched Friars from New London Street looking east towards the end of Fenchurch Street station. To the right is the side of St Olave's, Hart Street, the model for "St Ghastly, Grim" in Dickens' *The Uncommercial Traveller* with Seething Lane beyond. On the pavement is a cast-iron fire alarm pillar, once a common item of street furniture, now entirely vanished.

Opposite below: Crutched Friars, 20 June 1912
View looking west to Hart Street and Mark Lane from beneath the arch to Fenchurch Street railway station with railway offices to the right.

Bustling Bishopsgate

Left: 280-282 Bishopsgate, August 1912

Elaborate gilt and glass fascias were commonplace at this time. Saqui and Company is embellished with an ornate Art Nouveau shopfront, a curved glass entrance and mahogany display cases. The building above is a timber-framed 17th century house with a double-hipped clay tiled roof.

Above: 190 and 192 Bishopsgate, 22 August 1912

A fine pair of early 18th century town houses in mixed use. The floors over the Empire Restaurant are given over to a dental surgery advertising Allbrights Artificial Teeth. The small girl in the foreground appears to be wearing a high-crowned paper hat.

Dwelling fit for a king

Crosby Hall, Bishopsgate

One of the great private merchant's houses of mediaeval London, Crosby Hall was built between 1466-1475 for Sir John Crosby, whose tomb (1476) lies in the nearby Church of St Helen, Bishopsgate. In 1909 the great hall was dismantled and re-erected at Danvers Street, Chelsea Embankment under the supervision of Walter Godfrey for the British Federation of University of Women. In 1993 the Chelsea site was sold and the hall reverted to its original purpose as part of a magnificent neo-Tudor private residence for a City trader.

Left: Crosby Hall, 8 June 1907

The elaborate gabled frontage to Bishopsgate advertising The Palace of Richard III. Richard of Gloucester lived here at the time of the murder of the princes in the Tower.

Above: Crosby Hall, 8 June 1907

The magnificent 15th century carved oak roof and central lantern. The City arms and stencilled decoration are 19th century details. The frieze beneath the windows reads "For Good Digestion Wait on Appetite".

Lost inns and churches

**Left: Ye Olde Adam & Eve Inn,
264 Bishopsgate, 1907**

A fine timber-framed 17th century inn of a type once common in the City with a simulated rusticated stone facade and canted central bay. The weatherboarded gable retains one of its original 17th century leaded casements.

**Above: Church of St Alphage,
London Wall, c 1907**

This austere, monumental elevation of 1777 was remodelled in Gothic style in 1913, but the church was substantially destroyed in the Second World War. Only the remains of the 14th century tower of St Alphage, once part of the Chapel of the Priory of Elsyng Spital, survive.

**Opposite: Church of St Peter-le-Poer,
Old Broad Street, c 1905**

First mentioned in 1181, the church was rebuilt by the architect Jesse Gibson in 1792. In 1907 the parish was united with St Michael, Cornhill, and the church demolished for road widening. The pulpit, font and panelling were relocated to St Peter-le-Poer, Friern Barnet, which was built with the proceeds of the sale of the City site.

Venerable houses of the City

Above: 1-9 Finsbury Square, 2 September 1910
Although officially part of the Borough of Finsbury, and subsequently Islington, commercially Finsbury Square has been an important location for City businesses for generations given its proximity to Broad Street and Liverpool Street stations. This elegant symmetrical terrace designed in 1777 by James Peacock, the assistant to George Dance the Younger, stood on the west side backing onto the grounds of Honourable Artillery Company. Virtually the entire terrace was destroyed by enemy action in the Second World War.

Right: 1 Change Alley, Cornhill c 1910
In the early 18th century Change Alley was used as an open bourse frequented by speculators. It was the focus of the South Sea Bubble. Baker's Coffee and Chop House with its elegant twin-bowed frontage was typical of the small coffee houses where early City trading started. The London Missionary Society was founded here, after a particularly lavish meal, by eight non-conformist ministers on 4 November 1748.

Opposite above left: 37 Cheapside, 27 September 1908
Built in 1667-68, and still with its original casement windows, this was the earliest surviving example of a house erected immediately after the Great Fire. Beneath the second floor window is a carved tablet depicting The Chained Swan, the name of the tavern which once occupied the building.

Opposite above right: 43 Eastcheap, 22 August 1912
This evocative corner of the old City with its elegant early 19th century shop windows still survives remarkably unchanged. The house, which once formed part of a group of 17th century merchants' houses, abuts the side of Wren's St Margaret Pattens Church of 1684-87.

Opposite below: 8 Bow Churchyard, Cheapside, 30 August 1908
This splendid old 17th century house stood next to St Mary-le-Bow, Cheapside. Beneath the soft rubbed brick cornice the first and second floor windows are framed within eared brick panels. A curious young woman can be seen peering through the second floor window of the warehouse to the right

Haunting riverside stairs

Above: Knightrider Street, 16 May 1912
General view of Knightrider Street showing the Church of St Nicholas
Cole Abbey.

Right: 11 King Street, 23 March 1912
Small City retailers trading from the ground floor of an early Georgian
house with a City cab in the foreground. The poster behind the cab
for the Amateur Gardener offers advice on What to do in your garden
at Easter.

Opposite left: Trig Lane, 16 May 1912
View south to the river from Upper Thames Street with Trig Lane
Stairs and the chimneys of Bankside in the distance. Countless narrow
canyon-like alleys running down to the river and lined with
warehouses were a highly distinctive feature of Upper Thames Street
until its complete remodelling in the 1960s. Until 1835 and the
construction of King William Street, Fish Street Hill was the main
approach to London Bridge.

Opposite above right: 26-27 Fish Street Hill, Billingsgate, c 1913
Ramshackle 18th century houses supported by raking shores. No. 26
carries a royal crest over the shopfront. Evans's Stores provided
sundries for fishmongers at nearby Billingsgate Fishmarket.

Opposite below right: 18-19 Fish Street Hill, Billingsgate, c 1913
The produce suggests a general store catering for the particular
working needs of the Billingsgate Fishmarket with baskets for porters.

General Post Office, St Martin's-Le-Grand, 26 July 1911
Designed by Sir Robert Smirke and opened in 1829, the General Post Office was one of the most elegant buildings in London with a grand Greek Revival frontage. A new GPO building was opened on the site of Christ's Hospital in King Edward Street immediately to the west in the same year, and Smirke's landmark demolished.

Wren's lost masterpiece

Christ's Hospital, c 1906

Christ's Hospital was founded in 1552 on the site of the old Greyfriars Monastery and later rebuilt by Wren after the Great Fire incorporating the old Greyfriars cloisters. The Bluecoat school occupied a large area behind St Bartholomew Hospital between Giltspur Street and King Edward Street. In 1890 a Royal Commission recommended its removal from London and twelve years later it moved to Horsham. Samuel Taylor Coleridge, Leigh Hunt and Charles Lamb were all Bluecoat boys, Lamb recalling in later years how runaways were incarcerated in tiny dungeons and subjected to systematic chastisement. In spite of public indignation and strong opposition from the National Trust and the Society for the Protection of Ancient Buildings, the entire site was sold to the Post Office and levelled.

Above: Modelled on the chapel of King's College Cambridge, the main hall was designed by John Shaw Snr in 1825 in a romantic Tudor style. After Westminster Hall, the roof span was thought to be the largest in London without intermediate support. The hall was famous for its rats, which, attracted by the fragments of food, foraged about after dark in their hundreds.
It was a matter of pride for an "Old Blue" to catch them by hand, traps being considered cowardly.

Left: Part of the 17th century complex designed by Wren after the Great Fire with a fine carriageway of limestone setts.

Above: Goldsmiths' Company Hall, Foster Lane, 1913

The Goldsmiths' Company received its Charter in 1327 and in the 17th century it pioneered the use of promissory notes, the foundation of modern banking. The Hall, which still survives, was designed by Philip Hardwick between 1829-35 in a handsome Baroque style. The facade to Foster Lane is exposed in this view following the demolition of Smirke's General Post Office. The interior has a Roman altar to Diana discovered during the construction of the Hall in 1830, a chimneypiece from Canons Park reputedly by Roubiliac, and 17th century panelling, relocated from East Acton Manor House in 1912, along with a fine collection of plate.

Right: Apothecaries Hall, Blackfriars Lane, 16 November 1911

Apothecaries Hall dates from 1684 and was altered in 1779. The main buildings are of 1669-71 arranged around a central courtyard, parts of which rest on the mediaeval stone walls of the old Blackfriars monastery. The Pharmacy (shown here) is lined with traditional gilt and glass chemists' jars.

Hub of commerce

Opposite above: **St Paul's Churchyard, 21 June 1912**
East elevation from No. 7 Cheapside to Watling Street. View looking south towards the spire of St Augustine's Church. The east end of St Paul's Cathedral can be glimpsed to the right. Sorosis Shoes has a fine sinuous Art Nouveau shopfront and lettering.

Opposite below: **Old Change, 16 May 1912**
View south showing the intimate scale of the street. The carriageway is only wide enough for a single vehicle. To the left is Sorosis Shoe Shop. The spire of St Augustine's church is in the distance.

Above: **Junction of Old Change and Watling Street**
The south-east corner of St Paul's Churchyard viewed from the west with Cannon Street to the right and an elegant semi-circular block of Italianate offices in the foreground. The entire area was earmarked for clearance for St Paul's Bridge, a new Thames crossing, which was eventually abandoned. St Augustine Church (1680-83 by Wren) was destroyed in the Second World War, but rebuilt around surviving remnants as part of St Paul's Choir School.

London's library

Paternoster Row

To the north of St Paul's Churchyard was one of the great centres of the English book trade. Stationers and text writers sold religious and educational books as well as paternosters and graces, hence the name. By the early 18th century the book trade prevailed, supplanting mercers, silk and lace merchants and tire-men who sold "*top knots and other dressings for the female head*". "*By degrees ... learning ousted vanity, chattering died in to studious silence, and the despots of literature ruled supreme.*" The entire district was destroyed by enemy action on the night of 29 December 1940 along with six million books.

Above: 15 Paternoster Row, 18 August 1908
Samuel Bagster's Bible Warehouse with angled mirrors to each bay; a beautifully-detailed 18th century shopfront with a side entrance to Queen's Head Passage. Gas lanterns carry the street name and mark the entrances to side alleys.

Right: 51-52 Paternoster Row, 26 March 1912
View looking east showing the entrance to Paul's Alley. The London Bible Warehouse is on the right.

Opposite: 47 Paternoster Row, 17 August 1908
A fine late 17th century house that was typical of many in the area. The angled boards on the fronts of many of the houses are mirrors to reflect light into the windows above – once a common feature of the narrow alleyways of the City.

Dilapidated hostelries and working men's pubs

Above: Oxford Arms, Warwick Lane, 1875

"*Despite the confusion, the dirt and the decay, he who stands in the yard of this ancient inn may get an excellent idea of what it was like in the days of its prosperity when not only travellers in coach or saddle rode into or out of the yard, but poor players and mountebanks set up their stage for the entertainment of spectators who hung over the galleries or looked on from their rooms.*" (*The Athenaeum*: 20 May 1876) The Oxford Arms, one of London's most famous coaching inns, was situated at the end of a short lane leading out of the west side of Warwick Lane and was bounded to the west by the old City Wall. Rebuilt after the Great Fire, its first proprietor, Edward Bartlet, had "*a Hearse with all things convenient to carry a Corps to any part of England*". Its demolition in 1878 became a landmark in the development of the movement to preserve historic buildings.

Opposite above: The Old Blue Last public house, Dorset Street, 3 November 1904
An early Georgian facade and later ground floor frontage with applied lettering to the windows advertising popular brands of spirits.

Opposite below: "*Unlike the Paris cafe, which delights in the free sunshine of the boulevard, and displays its harmless revellers to the passers-by, the London tavern aims at cosiness, quiet and privacy*". (*Old and New London*, 1897)
A typical working man's public house interior. The first floor Club Room with gas lighting, plainly-detailed panelling and original chimneypiece with eared architraves.

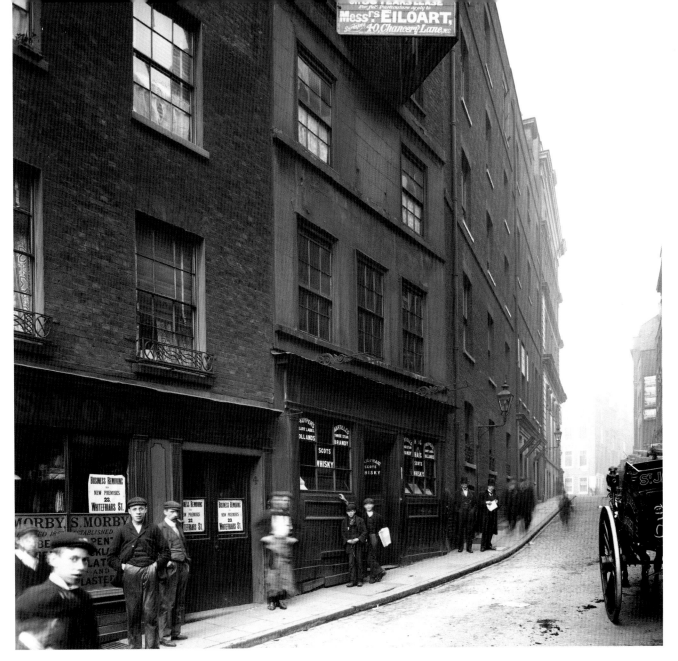

Above: 52 Gresham Street, 23 March 1912
Early 18th century house at the junction with Ironmonger Lane.

Opposite: 72 Leadenhall Street, 30 August 1909
The north side towards the eastern end. The Metropole building
appears to be an altered 17th century house with a central timber bay.
The curious slashes in the shop blind are probably to prevent water
collecting as run-off from the bay above.

Horse-drawn cacophony

Opposite: Ludgate Hill, c 1905
View looking south towards Ludgate Circus showing the railway bridge and signal gantries of the London, Chatham and Dover railway erected in 1865 in the face of public protest – "*a miracle of clumsy and stubborn ugliness*". To the right marked by a lavish array of barometer clocks is J W Benson, Steam Factory for Watches and Clocks. The elaborate coats of arms boast patronage by the ruling houses of Greece, Prussia, Russia and Siam with Queen Victoria's royal arms over the centre.

Above: 71-76 Fleet Street, 28 March 1912
A group of 18th and 19th century buildings in multiple use as newspaper offices, workshops, engravers and hairdressers, prior to clearance for street improvements. Signwriting and advertisement boards across the facades of buildings were commonplace until the introduction of controls over advertisements.

St Clement Danes Church, Strand
Above: 12 July 1906. View looking east from Newcastle Street showing the clearance of buildings by the LCC for the Holborn-Strand improvement scheme. The site in the foreground is now occupied by Australia House. The steeple of St Bride's, Fleet Street and the ethereal outline of St Paul's can be seen shimmering in the background haze.

Chapter Three

HOLBORN & STRAND

For centuries the Strand and Holborn-High Holborn were the principal historic routes westwards from the City of London to Westminster, but even after the removal of Temple Bar in 1878, congestion was severe. North-south movement was even worse with traffic confined to Chancery Lane or Drury Lane, or consigned to a convoluted maze of ancient streets between the two.

Planned for decades, the new Holborn to Strand road was the first and largest of the metropolitan improvements carried out by the newly-formed London County Council. The sheer scale of the project was immense – the most extensive clearance project undertaken in London since the Great Fire. Many of the images captured here were taken to record the neighbourhood on the eve of its destruction.

As well as eliminating traffic bottlenecks, the aim was to sweep away one of London's worst slums which lay between Drury Lane and Clare Market; a hotbed of criminal activity. A grand new Imperial boulevard – Kingsway – was created. This was linked to a massive sweeping crescent at its south end – Aldwych - beneath which ran a tunnel to accommodate the LCC's new electric trams. Gradually over 20 years the vacant plots were developed to a consistent design with elegant stone classical buildings housing offices, hotels, theatres and banks with space for new institutions, like the BBC at Bush House, and for the great halls of Empire, like Australia and India House.

The collateral damage was extensive. Whilst few mourned the loss of the squalid, if characterful, alleys off the Strand, or the infamous rookery around Clare Market, there was widespread dismay at the clearance of Holywell Street and Wych Street, which were regarded as amongst the most picturesque places in London; atmospheric rows of timber-framed buildings overhanging narrow streets imbued with a deep sense of antiquity. However, the enlightened decision to retain both St Mary-le-Strand and St Clement Danes was praised by contemporaries: evidence of growing concessions towards public interest in conservation. Some of London's most ancient Inns of Court fell victim too – Clements Inn, Danes Inn and New Inn were all swept away, and Clifford's Inn followed soon after.

Further north the last of the old coaching inns, like the Old Bell and the Black Bull in Holborn, were photographed on the brink of oblivion – rendered redundant by the railways and omnibuses of a new age, as motorised transport displaced the horse. In Bloomsbury the old Foundling Hospital at Corams Fields was still the focal point of the neighbourhood, but its days were numbered.

Westward along the Strand, change was more incremental as rows of older houses on individual domestic plots surrendered to much larger commercial buildings. The vast 1,000 room Hotel Cecil was one of the largest in the world when it opened in 1896 and the harbinger of things to come. Soon, Exeter Hall, that great bastion of radicalism, Cockerell's wonderful neo-classical Westminster Insurance offices, and, just to the south, the iconic Adelphi, were all to fall prey to a new generation of buildings designed to meet the needs of a new century.

The dignity of labour

Opposite: Strand – north side, c 1902
Demolition of buildings for the Holborn-Strand improvements. The photograph is carefully posed with the professionals – the surveyors and clerks of works – to the fore. The topmost advertisement on the hoarding behind offers a special express service to Paris in $7^1/_2$ hours.

Above: Strand, 14 April 1902
View from the south side looking west towards St Mary-le-Strand Church.

Right: 321-320 Strand, 11 June 1906
The north side of the Strand outside the west end of St Mary-le-Strand. The elegant cast iron drinking fountain was re-erected at Wimbledon Common.

Most extensive clearance

Above: 54-55 Lincoln's Inn Fields, 21 May 1906
Lincoln's Inn Fields, London's largest square, was laid out in the 1630s. This splendid pair of houses, erected by David Murray in 1640, are alleged to be by Inigo Jones. The pilasters to No. 54 were decorated with roses, fleur-de-lys and torches of Hymen to commemorate the marriage of Charles I and Henrietta Maria in 1625. Over the peculiar central arch were two stone tablets inscribed 'Duke Street 1648'. No. 54 was the house of the Sardinian ambassador. At the rear of the ground floor was a link to the Chapel behind to provide direct access into the ambassador's personal pew in the gallery.

Right: Sardinia Place, Holborn, 11 June 1906
View looking north into Sardinia Place with warehouses beyond.

Legal precincts

Clifford's Inn, Chancery Lane, 1903
Named after Robert de Clifford, who was granted the property by Edward II, an independent Inn was established by law students in 1345 and affiliated to the Inner Temple. The entire Inn was sold in 1903, when these photographs were taken, but it remained occupied until its demolition in 1935. Only the gateway survives.

Above: View of 1-9 Clifford's Inn
The elegant young woman is probably the secretary of the South American Missionary Society, which occupied the first floor of this range, which was built in 1682. Note the huge York stone slabs, cobbles and limestone setts to the courtyard.

New Inn, Strand, 1906
Founded in a converted tavern around 1460, New Inn lay north-west of St Clement Danes Church behind Wych Street, and was affiliated to the Middle Temple. In the 19th century membership declined and the entire Inn was acquired by the LCC in 1909 for the Holborn-Strand improvement scheme.

Right: New Inn Passage, Strand, 11 June 1906
View along New Inn Passage from Houghton Street. To the left is a Girls' Infants School, which explains the large numbers of children around the entrance to the corner shop.

Ramshackle survivors

Above: 13 Portsmouth Street, 5 May 1904
A truly remarkable survival of a modest 16th century house, which escaped demolition during the development of the area in the 18th century, and again with the Holborn-Strand improvements of the early 20th century. Its claim to be Dickens' 'Old Curiosity Shop' is entirely spurious, the name having been painted on the front to attract business to a dealer in books, paintings and old china in 1868.

Left: 8-11 Houghton Street, 5 August 1906
The hat shop at No. 9 advertises Gentlemen's Hats Polished for Sixpence. To the right, the jars over the shop fascia denote a hardware dealer selling oil for domestic use. The carriageway in the foreground is being relaid with a tarred wood block surface by 'The Improved Wood Pavement Company'. Wood blocks generated less noise than granite setts.

Opposite: 85-87 Fetter Lane, 21 July 1908
A surviving group of 17th century, timber-framed houses at the north end of Chancery Lane. The gabled building in the background, a fine Edwardian Art Nouveau composition by the architects Treadwell and Martin, still remains.

Quoting, quipping, quaffing

Wych Street was considered by many to be the most picturesque street in London and, for its size, it had the largest number of old houses, including many 17th century survivals.

Left: Wych Street, 21 June 1901
View of the east end with the north side of St Clement Danes Church in the distance.

The Rising Sun was a fine Elizabethan tavern, at the junction with Holywell Street. In the bar was a glass case containing a bone of Sir Thomas Armstrong who was hanged, drawn and quartered without trial for suspicion of involvement in the Rye House Plot, 1683. One of his quarters was fixed over Temple Bar. Dislodged in a high wind, it was brought to the pub as *"everlasting testimony to the lawlessness of the law"*.

Opposite: 38-48 Wych Street, 5 July 1901
"*There still remains some picturesque old patchwork buildings in and around Wych Street, Holywell Street and Drury Lane. Their picturesqueness largely relies on the varied and uncertain angles of tottering timbers, and the promiscuous arrangement of windows which protrude and overhang the little shops … Staircases lead to dingy rooms with hilly floors and blackened beams, running at all angles, drooping and groaning under the mingled weight of years and heavy tread*" (*Pall Mall Gazette*: 17 October 1889).

This well-known group of Jacobean survivors stood on the south side of Wych Street, but were swept away for the Holborn-Strand scheme.

Above: Holywell Street, 11 June 1906
"*Holywell Street was a wretched narrow lane … It was insanitary, physically as well as morally; at one time … it was the sink of iniquity; indecent literature and prints were always to be got there, and it took police many prosecutions to purify it … An attempt was made to change the name of the street into Booksellers Row, but the foul odour of Holywell Street still clung to it.*" (*Old Time Aldwych*: 1903).

The view looking west with demolition proceeding in the far distance.

Dilapidated rookeries

Opposite below left: Angel Court, c 1906
Angel Court was a narrow alley lined with 18th century dwellings which ran into Eagle Court.

Opposite above left: Drury Lane, 11 June 1906
The north side of Drury Lane looking east towards Wych Street in the distance. The narrow entrance to Harford Place can be seen marked by posters. The tiny children in the foreground show the single entrance to Nags Head Court, which is still in occupation even though the street frontage has been demolished.

Middle: Craven Buildings, 11 June 1906
Craven Buildings were erected in 1723 on part of the grounds of Craven House. At the end of the street was once a fresco of the Earl of Craven in armour, which was plastered over around 1813, but the panelled wall can be seen clearly in the distance. The undertaker's lantern on the extreme left advertises 'Funerals to Suit all Classes'.

Above: 1 Clare Market, 21 May 1906
Clare Market was notorious as "*one of those filthy, dilapidated rookeries that clung desperately to a sordid existence amid a changing environment*". It was well-known for its prize-fighters and as a hotbed of criminal activity, but "*a sort of romantic aura attached to the locality … from the old world air permeating the surrounding houses*".
(*Old Time Aldwych*, 1903).
The junction of Houghton Street and Clare Market. One of the oil jars over No. 11 Houghton Street can be glimpsed to the left.

Clinging to a sordid existence

Top: Denzell Street, c 1906
The junction of Denzell Street and Stanhope Street. The pub advertises a glass of gin for 4d. Opposite lies the pawnbrokers, which has relocated prior to demolition. Beyond Finch & Co on the right is the mixed Parochial School.

Above: 11 Sheffield Street, 3 May 1904
The dilapidated premises of M. Jewell, Waste Paper and Bottle merchants. The plaque on the front wall is a parish marker of St Clement Danes.

Opposite: Bear Yard, 11 June 1906
The Riland family, chimney sweep and carpet beater, outside their home at 12 Bear Yard.

C. RILAND
Practical
CHIMNEY SWEEP
& CARPET BEATER &c
12. Bear Yard Lincoln's Inn.

Above: Great Wild Street, Holborn, 11 June 1906
View looking south towards Sardinia Street. The young boy in the centre is holding two animal bones. Note the milk churn by the kerb.

Left: 55 & 56 Great Queen Street, Holborn, 1 June 1906
This half of a splendid town house erected in 1638 stood on the south side of Great Queen Street, and is attributed to John Webb, a pupil of Inigo Jones. First occupied by the Earl of St Albans, and later, briefly, by Sir Thomas Fairfax, it was acquired in 1684 by Lord Belasyse, by which time it had already been subdivided. The LCC plaque commemorates James Boswell, the biographer of Dr Johnson, who lived here until 1788. The two right hand bays have been tuck-pointed. The buildings were demolished for the new Freemasons Hall in 1927.

Opposite above: Little Queen Street, Holborn, 11 June 1906
Little Queen Street was swept away for the creation of Kingsway. To the extreme left is the side of the famous Holborn Restaurant.

Opposite below: Earlham Street, Seven Dials, c 1905
View of the north side of Earlham Street looking east with Seven Dials in the background showing the spontaneous street life which has been lost from so many parts of London.

Coaching inns on the road to Tyburn

The Old Bell Tavern and Hotel, Holborn, c 1897

Opposite: The frontage of The Old Bell dated from 1720, but the galleried portion at the rear where Shakespeare is alleged to have conducted one of his plays was built in 1521. Dickens and Thackeray were regulars.

Above: *"Passing through the ponderous wooden gates that have hung there for 300 years, visitors' attention is attracted by a row of bells for summoning chambermaids, boots, ostlers etc."*

Above: 116-117 Theobald's Road, Holborn, 19 December 1910
The last of the Holborn coaching inns showing the galleried courtyard to the rear with Bailey's covered vans in the foreground.

Right: Lamb's Conduit Passage, Holborn, 23 March 1912
View looking west along Lamb's Conduit Passage from the north-east corner of Red Lion Square. The corner building to the left of the picture was a mixed infants' school which accounts for the large numbers of children gathered outside in the rain. Conway Hall now occupies the north side of the passage.

Far right: 9 Eagle Street, Holborn, 8 April 1904
An early 18th century house with a refined pair of bowed shopfronts in use as a cheap lodging house. The boxes on the mullions to the first floor window are bird cages.

Above: 130 Strand, 22 April 1907

This fascinating photograph shows the development of commercial advertising in the early 20th century. The ground floor shopfronts follow the conventional late 19th century form with gilt and glass fascias and stall risers with applied lettering to the shop windows and floors above. The entire attic storey is covered by a painted signboard for *The Typhoon*, a production at the London Hippodrome, which boasted an arena that sank into a massive 100,000 gallon water tank for aquatic spectacles. The large Oxo sign heralds the arrival of electric advertisements which took little account of the architectural details of the buildings to which they were affixed.

Right: 413-415 Strand, 1914

This fine pair of 17th century houses situated next to the Adelphi Theatre with three storey projecting timber bays were typical of many which survived in the Strand until the early 20th century.

Refuge

Opposite below: Wesleyan Chapel, Great Queen Street, Holborn, 22 May 1906
Opened in 1817, the elegant Ionic portico of Welsh stone was added in 1840 beneath the fine tripartite north window. The chapel was demolished in 1910.

Opposite above: The Foundling Hospital, Guilford Street, Holborn, c 1912
The Foundling Hospital was established in 1742 by Captain Thomas Coram whose statue can be seen above the central stone niche. In the early days, abandoned babies were left here for the hospital to take in as foundlings, but due to the sheer level of demand a ballot system was introduced. The plainly-detailed buildings behind the entrance screen and lodges were laid out between 1745-53 by Theodore Jacobsen. Hogarth and Handel were both governors.

Above left: 20 Queen Square, Holborn, 19 October 1910
This spacious mid-18th century mansion in the north-west corner of the square was occupied by Louisa Twining, the philanthropist and poor law reformer and used as a refuge for the elderly and chronic epileptics. It was later the home of Thomas Henry Wyatt, President of the RIBA. At the time of its demolition for a hotel extension in 1960, it was in use as the Imperial Ladies Turkish Baths.

Middle left: Little Wild Street, Holborn, 11 June 1906
View looking north-east towards Sardinia Place. To the right is a remarkable group of original houses erected about 1690 with box gutters and timber balustrading to the front areas. Beyond is the Baptist Chapel and Mission Hall.

Below left: Featherstone Buildings, Holborn, 17 August 1908
Featherstone Buildings was a fine composition of two early 18th century terraces between High Holborn and Bedford Street. It was badly damaged by bombing and later demolished for post-war offices. Similar houses survive in Great James Street to the north of Theobalds Road. View of east side looking north.

Trafalgar Square, 31 July 1896

Panoramic view from the National Gallery looking south with the statue of General Sir Charles Napier to the right. In the background is a group of horse-drawn omnibuses.

Chapter Four

WESTMINSTER AND THE WEST END

Westminster was united by its very diversity. At its heart lay the government precinct with the great offices of state, many of which were moving out of the old aristocratic mansions into imposing new purpose-built edifices fit for modern government.

The ceremonial heart of London too was changing. Trafalgar Square is clearly recognisable, but its relationship with the Mall was transformed with the construction of Admiralty Arch and Aston Webb's remodelling of The Mall into an Imperial processional route culminating in the refaced frontage of Buckingham Palace.

Nash's Regent Street was poised to undergo complete reconstruction which took over 20 years to complete, whilst to the south the old aristocratic houses of Pall Mall were giving way to the opulent new gentlemen's clubhouses of St James's.

In sharp contrast, poverty was endemic in many areas. Some of the worst slums in London lay within a stone's throw of the Palace of Westminster, and to the west in Millbank.

At the heart of the West End amongst the glittering new shops, department stores, hotels and restaurants of Edwardian London, Soho retained its cosmopolitan character and raffish reputation.

Trafalgar grandeur

Above: Trafalgar Square, 31 July 1896

Panoramic view of Charing Cross. Le Sueur's famous statue of Charles I can be seen in the middle distance. Beyond the horse-drawn omnibus are the buildings at Charing Cross, soon to be removed for the creation of Mall Approach and Admiralty Arch.

Left: Trafalgar Square, 31 July 1896

Early morning view taken at 8.30am looking west from outside the Post Office on the corner of Morley's Hotel on the east side of the square. Note the shoeshine equipment at the pavement's edge. Behind the genteel group to the right is the statue of Major General Sir Henry Havelock, the hero of the relief of Lucknow, erected by public subscription in 1861. Such was the esteem in which he was held that on his death from exhaustion, the lights of all the ships in New York Harbour were dimmed on news of his passing. The posters announce the marriage between Prince Charles of Denmark and Princess Maud of Wales in the private chapel at Buckingham Palace on 22 July.

Opposite above: Admiralty Arch, Mall Approach, 21 November 1910

Admiralty Arch in the process of completion. Sir Aston Webb's remodelling of the Mall, Buckingham Palace and the completion of the Queen Victoria Memorial was one of the finest examples of grand axial planning in Europe, transforming the old ceremonial heart of London into a magnificent new Imperial capital.

Opposite below: Trafalgar Square, 14 February 1913

A pea-souper; photographed at 12.05pm looking towards the newly-completed Admiralty Arch in the distance. To the right, the houses in Charing Cross are being demolished for the new Mall Approach. London was renowned for its dense winter fogs – the product of the universal use of coal fires in houses and offices.

Facelift for Buckingham Palace

Above: **Buckingham Palace, 2 August 1913**

View of Blore's east front just prior to its refacing by Sir Aston Webb. The rond-pont of piers and gates surrounding the Queen Victoria Memorial is complete, but work has not started yet on the palace. To the left are the Australia Gates.

Left: **Buckingham Palace, 2 August 1913**

The east front of Buckingham Palace, built by Edward Blore between 1846-50, showing the centre and end pavilions enriched with allegorical sculpture and the much-criticised over-ornate centrepiece. Excoriated at the time for its ponderous design, it was refaced in 1913 by Sir Aston Webb in Louis XVI style to complement the Beaux-Arts replanning of the Mall and the Imperial iconography around the Queen Victoria Memorial.

Offices of state and empire

Top left: Great George Street, Westminster, c 1905
The north side of Great George Street comprised a handsome group of first-rate Georgian houses occupied by government offices and professional institutions. The whole street block was demolished for New Government Offices designed by J W Brydon between 1899-1915 in a confident neo-Baroque style to express British commercial and Imperial might.

Top right: Parliament Street, c 1909
Parliament Street Post Office at the junction with King Street looking south to Parliament Square. To the right of the picture clearance has started for the New Government Offices.

Above: Horseguards Avenue, Whitehall, 10 June 1912
This view from Horseguards Avenue towards the rear of Whitehall Gardens shows the Old War Office in the distance. The end house, No. 1 Horseguards Avenue, was built by Michael Angelo Taylor, the son of the architect Sir Robert Taylor, a prominent Whig MP and campaigner for improved paving and lighting. The canted bay to the rear of Pembroke House can be seen to the left.

The Westminster improvements

Above left: Parker Street, c 1905
View east along Parker Street towards Princes Street. The heart of old Westminster was notorious for its chronic poverty. Within 300 yards of the gates of the Palace of Westminster, Parker Street was typical of the squalor which was a standing rebuke to the national conscience until well into the 20th century. By 1905 these early 18th century terraces had fallen into use as cheap lodging houses

Below left: Millbank Street, 21May 1906
The west side of Millbank Street looking north with the Victoria Tower of the Palace of Westminster to the right: the largest square tower in the world when built. The houses are boarded up pending demolition and road widening.

Opposite above: Wood Street, 19 October 1909
The south-west corner of Wood Street at the junction with Tufton Street looking west. All are well-shod and most have hats or caps which suggests a group of respectable working families rather than the indigent for which the area was notorious. The entire neighbourhood was redeveloped between 1900-39.

Opposite below: Westminster Hospital, Broad Sanctuary, c 1910
Westminster Hospital stood opposite the Abbey and opened for patients in 1834. It was designed by W and H W Inwood between 1831-34 in a Tudor Gothic style and extended in the later 19th century. Originally it had room for over 100 patients, but only two baths, and drained into a cesspool. The hospital moved to Horseferry Road in 1939, but the building survived until 1951. The Queen Elizabeth II Conference Centre was built on the site between 1981-86.

Top: **Lambeth Bridge, Millbank, 8 June 1896**

Old Lambeth Bridge looking south from Millbank. Lambeth Palace and St Mary's, Lambeth can be seen to the left in the distance. The old narrow lattice-stiffened suspension bridge by P W Barlow was never successful and suffered from severe corrosion. A new Lambeth Bridge was completed in 1932 upstream of the old by the LCC's engineer Sir George Humphreys. The buildings in the foreground were pulled down for ICI's Nobel House (1927-29) and Thames House (1929-30), by Sir Frank Baines, one of the last expressions of late Imperial classical planning.

Above left: **Horseferry Road, Westminster, 21 May 1906**

The north side of Horseferry Road with the narrow entrance to Champions Alley to the right. Millbank was notorious for its poor housing plagued by damp and the perpetual threat of flooding from the Thames. On the night of 6 January 1928 fourteen people were drowned in the poorer areas next to the Thames when the river burst its banks. The Palace of Westminster was flooded and a section of the Embankment collapsed at Millbank.

Above right: **York Buildings, Westminster, 21 May 1906**

Living conditions in parts of Westminster were as bad as parts of the East End. By 1906 this squalid series of hovels was no longer fit for human habitation and had been given over to the storage of costermongers' barrows. Life in foetid courts like these must have been unbearable with little light or air. Whitewashing was common to increase reflected light.

Thameside curiosity

Above: Baltic Wharf, Millbank, 25 March 1909

Henry Castle & Son Shipbreakers Yard, with carved oak naval figureheads marking the south entrance. For many years these massive oak sentinels were a local landmark soaring high above the walls and gates of the yard. The carved arms over the gate are from HMS *Ocean* flanked by figureheads from HMS *Cressy* and HMS *Colossus*.

Right: The main entrance guarded by figureheads from HMS *Edinburgh* and HMS *Princess Royal* wth the legend "Britannia rules the waves" beneath. A ship's mast can be seen in the background. The yard was bombed in 1941 and its extraordinary collection of naval artefacts destroyed.

Regency elegance of Nash

Right: Shaftesbury Memorial Fountain, Piccadilly Circus, 1909

An atmospheric picture of the Shaftesbury Memorial Fountain (1886-93) by Alfred Gilbert with the winged figure of Anteros above; the first use of aluminium on a large-scale English monument. It rapidly became a London icon and the focus for flower-sellers and newspaper boys.

Above left: 44-48 Regent Street, 1910

Elaborate advertising attached to prominent buildings was a hallmark of the Victorian city, but in the 1890s illuminated lettering began to be introduced. By 1910 it was well-established on the north-east corner of Piccadilly Circus in spite of attempts by the London County Council to resist it. The first illuminated sign above fascia level was probably Mellins Pharmacy at number 48, but it was almost certainly unauthorised. The Crown Estate Commissioners resisted similar displays on the Criterion, Swan & Edgar and other adjacent buildings under their control through strict covenants.

Above right: 26-30 Regent Street, 23 November 1911

Railway booking offices on the east side of Regent Street close to the junction with Piccadilly Circus which can be glimpsed to the extreme left.

Top: Waterloo Place, St James's, c 1907

A remarkable view of Waterloo Place looking north to Piccadilly Circus showing Nash's original buildings with the Guards Crimea Memorial in the foreground and a complete absence of traffic.

Above: Regent Street, c 1910

Only once has a great plan for London been conceived and completed. The great metropolitan improvements of the Regency created a whole new spine through the centre of the West End and triggered a wave of northward expansion. Built as a personal speculation by John Nash between 1818-19, originally the Quadrant had continuous Doric colonnades running in a great curve from the projecting pavilions which can be seen (above). These were removed in 1848 to improve daylight and discourage vice.

View showing the Quadrant in 1910 prior to reconstruction. In the distance is a new office building breaking Nash's carefully orchestrated parapet line.

War Declared

Above: 83-89 Regent Street, 4 August 1914
There is little evidence that this was taken on the day Britain declared war on Germany. Life appears to continue as normal with the sandwich-boards promoting seaweed baths in Great Portland Street. To the left is the abrupt end of Norman Shaw's Piccadilly Hotel which triggered the complete reconstruction of the remainder of Regent Street as the leases progressively expired.

Middle right: 142-154 Regent Street, 1913
Originally Liberty's store stood on the east side of Regent Street south of the junction with Beak Street which can be seen to the left, before it relocated further north in the early 1920s.

Below right: 169-191 Regent Street, 9 October 1913
View of the west side with New Burlington Street to the left and a newly-completed office building in the distance breaking Nash's symmetrical composition.

Intersecting streets

Above: Oxford Circus, 19 October 1910
Oxford Circus was a pivot of Nash's great masterpiece as Regent Street ran north towards Portland Place.
View from the north-west side showing the juxtaposition of horse-drawn and motorised vehicles on setted street surfaces. The taxis boast swanky white-walled pneumatic tyres.

Right: 52 Wardour Street, Soho, c 1910
This elegant Regency shopfront with shallow bays to each frontage stood on the corner of Wardour Street and Old Compton Street until its demolition in the 1920s.

Nation of shopkeepers

Above: 34-39 Lisle Street, Soho, 26 July 1910

A fine terrace of late 18th century houses with a good run of contemporary shopfronts and a wealth of detail. The newsagents to the left has an enamel sign for the National Telephone Company to advertise a public telephone prior to the introduction of street kiosks. The placard for the *Mirror* leads with "Women watch for Dr Crippen". A similar terrace still survives on the north side now used by the Chinese community as shops and restaurants.

Right: 42, 43 & 44 St Martin's Lane, Covent Garden, 22 September 1910

An interesting group of early 18th century houses on the east side built by Thomas Parton in 1739, together with May's Buildings which can be seen to the right. In the foreground is a characteristic St Martin's in the Fields lamp column with delicate Art Nouveau detail. They are still in widespread use.

Above: 10-12 Coventry Street, Piccadilly, 17 March 1914

Lambert's, gold and silversmiths, proudly displays the royal warrants over a fine range of early 19th century shopfronts. Nos. 10-12 were demolished in 1920 for an extension of the Lyons Corner House which obliterated Arundell Street.

Right: St James's Market, Haymarket, 6 November 1908

St James's Market was built in 1663-66 to serve the newly-planned quarter around St James's Square. Rebuilt by Nash in 1817-18, the modest brick dwellings were levelled in 1916. The passageway in the distance led into the Haymarket.

Pennington Street, Tower Hamlets, December 1906
This long range of late 17th century dwellings stood directly opposite the enclosing wall and warehouses of London Dock. The poignant figures in the foreground were poor, but respectable. All are well-shod and most have hats or caps.

Chapter Five

THE EAST END

Cheek by jowl with the wealth of the City of London lay a completely different world – the East End: three square miles of densely-packed streets of terraced housing stretching east to the river Lea and shading imperceptibly northwards into the fringes of Hackney.

Over 1 million people from all corners of the earth were crammed into a labyrinth of streets, courts and alleys – a vast reservoir of cheap labour employed in casual work, sweated trades, or the Docks.

For the respectable poor home, was a rented room, or for the more fortunate, a house; for the less fortunate, a common lodging-house, the streets or the workhouse. It was a place of poverty, hardship, crime and degradation leavened only by an indomitable sense of humour and a deep-seated sense of community.

The river and the Docks continued to exert a powerful influence; the only escape from repetitive drudgery being the pub, which offered transient solace to those who could afford it; and for those who could, particularly for women, the risk of moral decline, many of whom descended from alcoholism to casual prostitution. The high population density supported a large number of small shops serving their local communities interspersed with workshops and small factories along the river and canals, or crowded into dingy backyards.

By 1900 some of the older trades, like silk weaving, were in sharp decline replaced by immigrants engaged in tailoring and the rag trade. Over 90% of the population of Stepney were immigrants or the children of immigrants, mainly East European Jews. Increasingly, radical improvements swept aside some of the worst slums, and the lives of many slowly improved, supported by charitable and philanthropic undertakings. The first Peabody block in London was in Commercial Street in 1864. Over 40 years later the LCC's Boundary Estate replaced the notorious slums around Old Nichol Street in Bethnal Green.

Pride in the docks

Above: East India Dock Road, Poplar, 1897

A commemorative arch raised to celebrate the 80th anniversary of All Saints parish. The arch is a replica of the West India Dock Gate, which was used as an emblem on the vestry mace in 1817. Street dressing for major royal or civic events was common at the time and popular in the East End.

Right: Ratcliff Cross Stairs, 4 February 1914

Once the Thames was approached through a myriad of stone causeways and stairs providing access between the warehouses to the river and its foreshore. Ratcliff Cross Stairs was typical. From here the great 16th century explorers embarked on their voyages to the Arctic and elsewhere.

In the 13th century lime burning began in kilns and oasts, known as "*lymostes*" at the mouth of an insanitary creek called the Black Ditch. By the mid-16th century the entire district was known as Limehouse. By the 1880s it was Chinatown, home to large numbers of Chinese and Lascar sailors and migrants, with an unsavoury reputation for illicit opium dens and Chinese criminal gangs in the area around Pennyfields.

Opposite below: 89-95 Ropemakers Fields, Limehouse, c 1900

The eastern end of Ropemakers Fields at its junction with Nightingale Lane. The left-hand pair of early 18th century houses have once-elegant Georgian shopfronts, No. 89 with an elegant double bow. George Morrow and Son was a scull and mast maker; James Barnett, next door, a ship chandler offering canvas, rope fend-offs, lamp glasses and oakum for both river and canal trade. Two of the three children have no shoes – a sign of abject poverty.

Opposite above: 93-101 Three Colt Street, Limehouse, c 1900

Textures of the past. This remarkable street scene epitomises London at the dawn of the 20th century with stone pavements, setted streets and small local shops in old vernacular buildings. Weatherboarded houses were once common in inner London, but today only a few fragments remain. Siebert's, with its queue of children outside a well-stocked shop window, was one of two German bakers in the street.

Lost lustre

Left: 65-79 Cambridge Road, Mile End, 14 November 1910

An interesting survival of a late 17th century terrace with tiled roofs and dormer windows. The right hand end has been divided into mean lodging houses with brick screen walls to the front steps.

Above: 168 Cambridge Road, Mile End, 15 October 1903

A typical East End street scene with modest two-storey artisans' houses and shops, a setted street and tramlines. W T Maughan was a wholesale and retail confectioner operating from a small yard next to the store.

**Above: 215-223 Bow Road, Bow,
19 November 1909**

A fine group of buildings of various periods just east of St Mary's Church. The houses to the extreme left and right still stand, but the remainder have been swept away, including the impressive, eight-bay Georgian facade to Anderson's.

Left: 236-238 Bow Road, Bow, 18 April 1899

The teeming neighbourhoods of high-density housing in the East End supported a huge number of local businesses and shops. Milo's Dining Rooms offered a Good Pull Up for Carmen, whilst Bailey's Chemist next door with a display of traditional apothecaries' jars in the window offered Dr Collis Brown's Chlorodyne.

**Left: 242A-244 Bow Road, Bow,
18 April 1899**

Inner London as it was once. The old tiled roof suggests the refronting of an older building in the early 19th century. Note the Venetian blinds to the first floor windows. The placards outside Hockley's show a moment frozen in time, *The Golden Penny* offered a History of Liverpool Football Club; *The Sun*, "Shocking Discovery at Broad Street Station" to the right of which stands the ghostly trace of a young girl.

**Above: 52 Dace Road, Old Ford
8 December 1904**

F Crook's local corner shop with a splendid array of enamel advertisements promoting a whole range of products, most of which are familiar today.

Teeming neighbourhoods with small shops

Above: 75-77 Broadway, London Fields, 16 October 1906

The dogs seem more interested in Rosenberg's the family butcher rather than the dog food shop next door, which has a finely-detailed canted bay shopfront coruscated with colourful enamel advertisements.

Right: 85 Broadway, London Fields, 16 October 1906

P J Ryan, tobacconists, with a fascinating amount of contemporary detail. The advertising lantern is angled to throw light onto the shop window which advertises Victory V gums and Fry's chocolate. The *Daily Mirror* announces a major mine disaster in Durham with 30 killed and 150 entombed. The poster above the neighbouring shop offers the entire street block for immediate redevelopment, but similar parts of Broadway still exist.

Lifelines for the poor of the parish

Above: 9 Gainsborough Road, Hackney Wick, 29 May 1909

Pawnbrokers were a common sight across London and their regular use a way of life in the East End. Edwin Brigham was typical, offering short-term loans against items of value. The window is crammed with clocks, vases, watches and silver, whilst the crowd milling outside shows that there was no shortage of business.

Right: Aldermanbury Almshouses, 52-60 Philip Street, Shoreditch, c 1910

Local tradition alleged that the curious stone house to the left of the picture was built with stone from old London Bridge. This was probably true as a stone tablet inside the party wall stated it was built in 1817 by Mr Malcott, who also built Old Bridge House, 54 Streatham Hill (demolished 1928) utilising stone from the bridge, hence the name.

Above: 209-213 Mare Street, Hackney, 13 May 1904

A short terrace of early 18th century cottages with the gable end covered with contemporary posters. The children in the foreground in caps and high collars look particularly stylish.

Right: 1-5 Westgate Street, Hackney, 28 October 1904

The large early Georgian house with the grand pedimented doorcase would have been occupied originally by a merchant of some substance. By the time of the photograph, it was in use as the Triangle Home for Working Men. It was commonplace for once genteel houses to be divided into rooms and lodgings as the social composition of districts changed, and fashionable society moved elsewhere.

An eccentric city
of unexpected delights

Above left: 336 Old Street, Shoreditch, c 1910

This resplendent gilded cockerel, implausibly attributed to Grinling Gibbons, once adorned The Cock public house in Fleet Street, haunt of Pepys, Thackeray, Dickens and Tennyson, until 1887 when the building was demolished for the Bank of England Law Courts Branch. Tennyson wrote of it:

> The Cock was of a larger egg
> Than modern poultry drop,
> Stept forward on a firmer leg,
> And cramm'd a plumper crop

Edward Maund, a joiner and shopfitter, acquired the bird and gave it pride of place in a niche on the front of his premises in Old Street, where it became a local landmark.

Above right: 11 Pitfield Street, Shoreditch, c 1905

This ancient late 17th century house with a mixed pantile and clay tile roof and timber eaves cornice was a hardware shop. The engaged oil jars denote a dealer in oils. The shop window is stacked with Sunlight and Lifebuoy soaps. The bakers to the left has a display of Peek Freans and Huntley & Palmers biscuit boxes.

Right: Queen Square, Finsbury Avenue, Shoredirch, c 1905

Situated on the northern fringe of the City of London, Queen Square was a narrow courtyard of early 18th century houses off Finsbury Avenue, close to Broad Street Station. W H Brooks, a chimney sweeper and carpet beater, poses outside the grand pedimented doorcase to the house, which has fallen on hard times.

Opposite: Thatched Cottage, Spring Hill, Clapton, 26 February 1912

This quaint little thatched cottage was probably built on common land in the late 18th century. It was used as John Such's refreshment rooms next to Pink's Nurseries, until it was burnt out in 1919.

Shad Thames, c 1910.

Much of the river was lined by vertiginous warehouses creating dark canyons separated by slit-like alleys leading to ancient stairs, jetties and wharves. At Shad Thames a myriad of iron bridges spanned the street to allow goods to be moved across the walkways to warehouses inland.

Chapter Six

SOUTH OF THE THAMES

South London was always the capital's backyard – a service area for the Cities of London and Westminster across the river. In the Middle Ages Southwark was London's red-light district, with theatres, inns, bull-and bear-baiting rings, but it was relatively isolated – hence the soubriquet "London-over-the-water" – and its administration confused. Its development was unlocked first by the construction of a series of new bridges – Vauxhall (1816), Waterloo (1817) and Southwark (1819) – which triggered major new road improvements, such as St George's Circus and Blackfriars Road, and later by the arrival of a congeries of railways.

In 1900 river-borne trade and industry dominated the northern edges in a huge arc along the Thames in a chaotic jumble of vertiginous warehouses, wharves, printing works, sawmills, factories and breweries. Many industries, like white lead works, were highly toxic, slowly poisoning the workforce. Noxious trades were widespread including bone-boiling, cat-gut making, fish-smoking and leather tanning. Large numbers of costermongers and street traders working from handcarts operated from here. Bankside was one of the principal sources of London's power with the old Phoenix Gas Works, an electricity generating station and the pumping station of the London Hydraulic Power Station all housed on the site later occupied by Bankside Power Station.

Borough High Street retained much of its mediaeval street plan and grain with dozens of narrow passages and alleys running off the main frontage interspersed with ancient coaching inns and an unwholesome reputation for poverty and crime. It was here that Charles Booth found the worst extremes of deprivation and squalor close to the old Marshalsea Prison.

As London expanded outward it absorbed many older, outlying settlements such as Clapham, Rotherhithe, Camberwell, Peckham and Greenwich. The new suburbs created were often rigorously socially stratified with subtle nuances of class and wealth ranging from the genteel through various gradations of the middle and working classes to slum districts full of cheap lodging-houses. The bewildering shifting dynamic of London's neighbourhoods oscillating between the fashionable and the downwardly mobile remains a constant feature of London's history which persists to this day.

Crossing the great divide

Above: Pool of London, c 1914

Panoramic view of the Pool of London showing the river crowded with shipping. The tower of the Church of St Magnus the Martyr is in the centre of the picture with the Monument to the right. The vast mass of Cannon Street train shed obscures the view of St Paul's which can be seen in the haze on the horizon.

Left: Tower Bridge, c 1893

The need for a new river crossing was identified as early as 1879. Authorised by an Act of Parliament in 1885, it was designed by the City Corporation architect, Sir Horace Jones and the engineer, John Wolfe Barry as a bascule bridge to allow the passage of large ships into the Pool of London. The Act stipulated a clear span of 200ft, a height of 135ft and the use of the Gothic style to harmonise with the Tower of London. Tower Bridge opened in 1894 and rapidly became a London icon. The new Tower Bridge Approach Road required extensive demolition on the north bank.

The iron frame and upper level walkway can be seen here rising from the great stone bastions sunk into the river.

Hemmed in by high walls

Above: Marshalsea Prison, Southwark, 14 September 1908

View of the rear of the former Marshalsea Prison from the burial ground behind showing the spiked fence to the old exercise yard. In 1824, Charles Dickens' father was imprisoned for debt in the Marshalsea. In 1842 it was closed and the buildings were used as a factory.

"*It was an oblong pile of barrack building, partitioned into squalid houses standing back to back, so that there were no back rooms; environed by a narrow paved yard, hemmed in by high walls, duly spiked at top*".

(Charles Dickens, *Little Dorrit*)

Left: Little Dorrit's bedroom, 22 September 1908

Dickens frequently based his books on actual places he knew. Much of the early story of Little Dorrit revolved around the Marshalsea. Here, Little Dorrit was born and took lodgings with her godfather in the "*turnkey's sky parlour*" – a bleak garret room – so she could care for her father, brother and sister. This extraordinary photograph shows her home.

Wretched remains...

Above: 309-315 Borough High Street, c 1903

A classic group of 17th century houses with projecting central bays and horizontal sash windows to the gables. The picture eloquently portrays the extraordinary range of details commonly found in the Edwardian high street – elegant signwriting, gilt and glass fascias, applied lettering to shopfronts and spectacular ornamental ironwork. Angled lanterns, which were suspended from fascias and designed to throw light back onto shop window displays, have now vanished from London's streets.

Right: The Old Farm House, Disney Place, Borough, 17 February 1910

"*There is probably no more picturesque building left standing in London-Over-the-Water than the ancient residence known as the Farm House*" (*Daily Chronicle*, 9 January 1914)

The old Farm House was a remarkable survival tucked away at the end of a cul-de-sac and may have been a remnant of a 16th century house built for the Earl of Suffolk. It fell into use as a doss-house and paupers of many parishes were farmed out here – hence the name. For a while it was the lodging of the Welsh tramp poet, W H Davies, who wrote and published *The Soul's Destroyer and other Poems* from here. Dickens knew it well.

The brackets to the elaborate 17th century door canopy are still in place, but its roof has gone. The spectral figure of a young girl can be seen inside the doorway.

Warren of sunless courts

Top: Moss's Alley, Bankside, 16 May 1912
View looking north from the junction with Ladd's Court – a bleak harsh world of hard unremitting grind with the mark of poverty stamped indelibly both on the faces of the people and the houses.
To the left the chalk marks read Chocolate Club Held Here. The child to the right seems intent on throttling a kitten. His mother seems prematurely old, but is probably less than 30.

Above: Ladd's Court
Ladd's Court viewed from Pitt Place with Moss's Alley running from left to right. The sheer number of people gathered shows the chronic overcrowding. 1, 800,000 people in London lived on or below the poverty line with a further 1,000,000 with just one week's wages between subsistence and pauperism. Life was poised precariously between respectability and destitution.

Right: Taylor's Yard, Bankside, 16 May 1912
View from Moss's Alley into Taylor's Yard with the walls of the adjacent saw mills beyond.

Melancholy streets in a penitential garb of soot...

Above left: 24-26 Jacob Street, Bermondsey, c 1910
Timber houses were built in Bermondsey and Southwark using a ready supply of wood from nearby wharves, long after they were proscribed in the Building Act of 1707. These old 18th century houses with massive central chimney stacks were once part of the infamous rookery of Jacob's Island, the setting for Bill Sikes' death in *Oliver Twist*; but by 1910 the area was much changed. The houses seem well cared-for and the occupants relatively respectable.

Above right: 156-162 Long Lane, Bermondsey, 6 February 1913
A splendid display of contemporary posters and advertisements on a mixed group of buildings at the south-west end of Long Lane. No. 158 and the cottages to the left are boarded up awaiting redevelopment together with a large vacant plot at the rear.

Right: Grange Walk, Bermondsey, c 1905
Grange Walk stands on the site of Bermondsey Abbey, of which fragments still remain. In the 18th century the brick houses with carved doorcases beyond would have been occupied by prosperous merchants, but as the area declined they fell to multiple occupation.

Isolated riverside village

Above: 298-312 Rotherhithe Street, Rotherhithe, 8 November 1911

An atmospheric view of Rotherhithe Street with St Paul's Lane entering from the right in the middle distance. William Corney's stores has a fine shallow, double-bowed shopfront. Beyond are late 17th century timber-framed houses with weatherboarded walls.

Sea captains and merchants

Above: Mayflower Street, Rotherhithe, 16 May 1914
Mayflower Street (formerly Princes Street) was built in 1721-23 as grand houses with a variety of plan forms for sea captains and merchants. Once a gated street, it fell on hard times and by 1914 was in multiple occupation as lodging houses. Much of the street survived the war, but what remained was swept away in the mid-1950s.

Left: 242 Rotherhithe Street, 8 November 1911
An 18th century survivor sandwiched between two later buildings. The house is in poor condition, the windows broken and the weatherboarding held in place by straps.

Artisans' quarters

Above: 69-79 Nine Elms Lane, Vauxhall, 24 August 1908
A short row of six small artisans' houses dating from the early 18th century with large central chimney stacks and pantiled roofs, once typical of inner south London.

Middle right: Brune Place, Newington Butts, Elephant & Castle, 26 November 1911
The cottages at the end of the court are marked with a plaque – Rose Court 1708 – but the remainder are later, 19th century terraces. Those to the left are more generous than most with small front yards for drying washing. The woman in the foreground is heavily pregnant, but all appear to be tired, worn out and depressed.

Below right: 20-23 High Street, Lambeth
Lambeth High Street was a busy working neighbourhood coloured by its proximity to the river. Ship chandlers and maritime suppliers were widespread; Leaver and James, mast scull and oar makers, were typical. Compare this view with the later photograph taken in 1923 on p135.

Euston Arch, 1934

An heroic monument to Britain's railway age. This huge Greek Doric propylaeum, built in 1838 to the design of Philip Hardwick, rose over 70ft to form a gigantic gateway to Euston, the first mainline terminus in a capital city anywhere in the world. Its demolition in 1962 triggered a public outcry which did much to boost the growth of the conservation movement and popular reaction against the institutional philistinism which characterised the post-war period.

Chapter Seven

LONDON'S ZENITH 1918-39

The end of the First World War marked a watershed for London and the dawn of a new age. The population grew by 1.2million in 20 years. Mortality rates fell. Living standards improved and even working class families were able to acquire new luxury commodities, and enjoy new forms of entertainment, like the cinema, radio and gramophone. Increasingly, the chronic poverty which had stalked the Victorian and Edwardian capital was consigned to the past, even if areas of relative deprivation persisted, particularly in the East End, where, in spite of slum clearance and campaigns to improve child health and education, large numbers of London's poor remained trapped.

Rising land values, new transport infrastructure and population growth fuelled the greatest development boom in London's history. Central London was transformed as offices, department stores, hotels, underground stations, cinemas and huge blocks of flats replaced familiar four-storey houses and terraces. Pre-war trends resurfaced with renewed vigour. The redevelopment of Kingsway and Regent Street resumed. The West End consolidated its position as London's great shopping and entertainment centre, whilst many of the old aristocratic mansions of Mayfair gave way to modish new flats and offices. Besieged by developers, London's garden squares were given statutory protection in 1931 in one of the most enlightened pieces of planning legislation ever devised – ensuring a long term future for one of its most distinctive elements and crucial to its sense of place.

The defining characteristic of the inter-war period was the growth of the suburb, driven by the relentless expansion of the transport network. Between 1918-1939 London underwent astonishing spatial expansion. Over 860,000 houses were built in Greater London predominantly in outlying areas for the new middle classes. London's old peripheral villages like Eltham, Carshalton, Stanmore and Enfield were engulfed by a centrifugal tide of low-density development, whilst wholly new suburban communities were built from scratch in a variety of whimsical, and often playful, vernacular and traditional styles. Much derided, London's suburbs remain one of its most notable characteristics – home to over 70% of its population. By 1939 one in five of the people of England and Wales was a Londoner.

Without question, in 1939 London was still the sovereign of cities, the greatest city in the world – its largest port, its largest bank, its largest workshop and the capital of the British Empire. It dominated its hinterland, which embraced the whole of south-east England, but with such a concentration of population, wealth and commerce into just 610 sq miles, it was also shockingly exposed – an unparalleled strategic target wide open to new forms of warfare and, ominously, mass air attack.

Birth of a new era

Above: Old County Fire Office, Piccadilly Circus, November 1924

Nash's Old County Fire Office in the process of demolition. After much protracted wrangling, it was replaced by a similar handsome arcaded frontage by Sir Reginald Blomfield with massive chimney stacks framing an oval dome designed to terminate the east side of the Quadrant and close the vista from Lower Regent Street.

Left: Swan & Edgar, Piccadilly Circus, November 1924

The shallow curve of Swan & Edgar's department store shortly before reconstruction commenced. To the left the step-change in scale generated by Norman Shaw's Piccadilly Hotel can be seen clearly. This dictated the form, bulk and scale of the subsequent redevelopment of the whole area.

Above: View showing the uncomfortable collision of scale between the south-west curve of the Quadrant and the old curve of the Circus. Blomfield's reconstruction created a magnificent new frontage to the west side of the Circus, squaring off the entire junction in a monumental classical composition with huge concave-curved roof pavilions crowned by gilded pineapple finials.

Right: Savile Place, c 1933

In a pale reflection of the Burlington Arcade, which was under construction to the south, in 1818 eight tiny shops were inserted into the walls of Savile Place, reputedly the smallest shops in London. Of the original retailers, a stick shop and cobbler's stall survived until this delightful thoroughfare was demolished in 1937.

Keeping watch

Above: The Old Watch House and Court House, Marylebone Lane, 1935

Built on the site of an old plague pit, the Old Watch House was built in 1804 for five watchmen who made day and night patrols of the parish. The adjoining Court House opened in 1825. Over the door of the Watch House are the arms of the Harley family, dated 1729. With the construction of the new Town Hall in Marylebone Road, the buildings were sold and used briefly as a bookshop, before they were demolished in 1935.

Left: 51-53 Broadwick Street, Soho, c 1935

Formerly No. 36, by the 1930s this once-spacious early 18th century house had been converted into tenements. The original ground floor rooms and entrance passage were converted into shops, an open passage inserted at the western end, and another tenement block crammed into the rear courtyard.

Above: Chesterfield House,
South Audley Street, Mayfair, May 1932
Set back from the street behind high walls and a grand arcaded courtyard, Chesterfield House was designed by Isaac Ware for Lord Chesterfield between 1747-52. It was regarded as one of the finest aristocratic town houses in London with a spectacular French rococo interior. From 1894 the house was owned by the brewer, Lord Burton. In 1922 it became the home of the Princess Royal before it was sold and demolished in 1937.

Right: 29-32 Petty France, Victoria, c 1930
To the right is a pair of late 17th century houses with timber box cornices. To the left is a pair of early 18th century houses. All have fallen on hard times and are indicative of the dilapidated condition of much of central Westminster well into the 20th century. A lucrative trade operated in architectural salvage.

Lost mansions

Above: Norfolk House, 31 St James's Square, 1932
Designed by Matthew Brettingham between 1748-52 for the ninth Duke of Norfolk, the Palladian style was inspired by Holkham Hall with a long frontage of nine bays enriched with stone dressings. Together with Chesterfield House, it was renowned for its lavish French rococo interior, one of the earliest in London. Regarded by the LCC as having only limited architectural merit, it was demolished in 1939, although the music room was salvaged and re-erected at the Victoria & Albert Museum.

Right: View of the Salon, or Ballroom which was redecorated in Louis Quinze style in 1845 with papier-mache and carton pierre enrichment and sumptuous gilt-framed mirrors. In the panel over the door is a ducal coronet and scrolled monogram bearing the initials H and C over an N with a gilded plaster ceiling of geometrical circles above. The room is laid out with some of the contents of the house prior to sale.

Above: **Dorchester House,
Park Lane, c 1927**
Designed by Lewis Vulliamy, as a massive
town house for the millionaire, R S
Holford, Dorchester House was regarded as
the finest private house in London and the
home of its best art collection. It was built
between 1851-57 and modelled on the
Palazzo della Farnesina in Rome. Later it
was occupied by the American ambassador,
William Whitelaw Reid, but with rising
land values in the post-war period it was
pulled down in 1929 to make way for the
jazzy new Dorchester Hotel designed by
Curtis Green.

Right: **Devonshire House, Piccadilly,
October 1920**
After a disastrous fire in October 1733, the
third Duke of Devonshire commissioned
William Kent to design a new mansion which
stood behind a high wall facing Piccadilly.
Much criticised for its external austerity, the
interior provided an opulent setting for an
extensive art collection including works by
Tintoretto, Titian and Rembrandt. The large
rear garden was separated from the rear garden
of Lansdowne House to the north by
Lansdowne Passage.

Above: High Row, 68-92 Knightsbridge, 1931
View of the north side of Knightsbridge immediately to the west of the Hyde Park Hotel which can be seen on the extreme right. These once-grand houses overlooking Hyde Park were bought for redevelopment in the 1930s, but remained empty until their demolition in December 1942. Bowater House was built on the site in 1956-58. The plaque on No. 70 marks the home of Charles Reade, the novelist and playwright who lived there from 1867-82.

Middle left: Chelsea Bridge, c 1930
An evocative period photograph of Chelsea Bridge from the south approach. On the right, note the woman and child with perambulator; to their left is an LCC tram stop for the 32 to Lavender Hill and Clapham: the tram tracks stop abruptly here. At the left of the picture is a delivery van.

Leftt: 11 Clements Inn Passage, 7 February 1927
A superb atmospheric view of Ye Olde St Clements Inn Restaurant, an old 17th century gabled house with a fine 18th century shopfront, which survived the huge Holborn to Strand Improvement scheme, but succumbed to later development.

On the eve of destruction

Above left: Clifford's Inn, c 1932
View of Clifford's Inn and a local resident. 24 years after it was sold and the images on p108, it remained in occupation until it was pulled down in 1935.

Serjeants Inn, 1932
Serjeants Inn occupied the site immediately west of Clifford's Inn, to which it was connected, with a frontage to Chancery Lane, which had been occupied as early as 1425. As late as 1860 part of the pavement of the inn was flagged in stone taken from old St Paul's, and it retained oil lamps long after the introduction of gas.

Above right: View of the south-west corner. To the left beneath the porch are the offices of the Colonial and Continental Church Society.

Right: View of north-east side of the square showing some of the elegant early 18th century terraced houses designed by Robert Adam for offices and lawyers' chambers. To the right the grand stone frontage, also by Adam, was used by the Church of England Sunday School Institute.

A city reborn

Opposite above: Bush House, Aldwych, c 1932
Brave new world. View of Bush House at the centre of the great axial vista south from Kingsway, but prior to the completion of its wings. In the distant haze beyond is the facade of Somerset House. The Holborn to Strand improvements incorporated an underground tramway tunnel, the entrance to which can be seen in the foreground.

Opposite below left: George Court, Strand, c 1935
George Court at the junction with York Place. Note the bird cages in the open window high above the passage entrance.

Opposite below right: 39-59 Strand, November 1924
The Strand in its heyday with domestic-scaled buildings of various periods on their original mediaeval plots and a wealth of fascinating detail.

Right: 76 Bartholomew Close, Smithfield, 1927
Early 18th century houses. The small windows denote houses with front staircases – an early plan-form.

Above: The London Institution, Finsbury Circus, 1936
View showing demolition works in progress in 1936. Founded in 1806, the London Institution moved to this elegant neo-classical building on the north side of Finsbury Circus in 1819. Designed by William Brooks, it boasted a fine pedimented portico carried on four fluted Corinthian columns over a Greek Doric porch. Intended "for the Advancement of Literature and the Diffusion of Useful Knowledge", it was a lecture hall and later the home of the School of Oriental Studies. Note the careful way in which the K2 telephone kiosk has been sited – framed between the Doric columns of the left-hand bay.

Opposite above: 32-34 Tower Hill, c 1920
This once elegant late 18th century building stood north-east of the Tower with Eastminster (formerly King Street) beyond to the left. The flank elevation and box cornice of No. 1 Eastminster are clearly visible.

Opposite below: 1-3 Eastminster, Tower Hamlets, 22 November 1920
A remarkable survival of a short row of late 17th century houses retaining their original bracketed timber box gutters, flush-framed sashes and steeply-pitched clay tile roofs. The iron bollards mark the boundary between the City of London and Tower Hamlets.

Above: Moneyer Street, Shoreditch, 1931
As early as the 17th century Hoxton was renowned for its market and nursery gardens, and related trades continued well into the 20th century. Columbia Road market is still a mecca for gardeners and enthusiasts.
View showing north end of Moneyer Street, Hoxton, with carts piled high with plants, shrubs and saplings.

Middle right: 48 Hoxton Square, 1921
View of the south side. Hoxton Square, built in the 1680s, was home to one of the first Dissenters' Academies. By 1902 it was synonymous with poverty, overcrowding and crime, characterised by Charles Booth as "*the leading criminal quarter of London, and indeed of all England*" – the home of the pickpocket, 'whizzer' or 'dip', and gangs of shoplifters or 'hoisters'. It is now one of London's coolest neighbourhoods, a centre for creative industries and nightlife.
Although bombed heavily, some of the original houses survived into the 1970s. Today only a handful remain.

Below right: Crooked Billet Yard, Kingsland Road, Hackney, 1933
A fascinating view of a short row of 17th century cottages with an external staircase to the first floor entrance beside which a communal privy has been built with a timber modesty screen.

The awful East

Opposite above: Lynedoch Street, Shoreditch, July 1920

The City of Dreadful Monotony. Each house shoulder to shoulder with its neighbour, two storeys high and 18ft wide; street after street of grimy buildings against a slate-coloured sky. Yet beneath the drab exterior lay vibrant working class communities offering each other help and support in times of acute need.

Opposite below: Provost Street, Shoreditch, 1931

"No more dreary spectacle can be found on this earth than the whole of the awful East ....the colour of life is grey and drab. Everything is helpless, hopeless, unrelieved and dirty ....and the rain, when it falls, is more like grease than water from heaven. The very cobblestones are scummed with grease." (Jack London, *People of the Abyss*)

View of Provost Street prior to its demolition in 1931.

Above: 64 Red Lion Street, Wapping, 1928

A bleak, rain-sodden view of the Old George public house. Red Lion Street was slated for demolition in 1929, but a number of the houses are still occupied. Note the ubiquitous chalk marks on the walls.

Right: View of the derelict outhouse and rear yard.

Old vernacular houses in forgotten village cores

Above: 7-15 Blue Anchor Lane, Peckham, 1928
An old range of 18th century weatherboarded cottages boarded up prior to demolition.

Middle right: 20-23 High Street, Lambeth, 1923
By 1923 Lambeth High Street was becoming progressively down-at-heel and ripe for the comprehensive redevelopment that was soon to eradicate its distinctive identity as an ancient riverside neighbourhood.

Below right: 37 St Mary Church Street, Rotherhithe, December 1934
This early 18th century cottage stood to the west of St Mary's Rotherhithe, at the junction with Elephant Lane, which led through to Elephant Stairs on the river. The weatherboarded passage to the left connected with Princes Street (later Mayflower Street).

Opposite above: Waterloo Road, c 1930
Dilapidated stucco buildings at the junction of Waterloo Road and The Cut.

Opposite below: 91-97 Three Colt Street, Limehouse, c 1923
Three of the five weatherboarded houses shown in the Edwardian photographs on p99 can be seen here in an advanced state of decay, the wooden gable wall supported by a single prop. Two are derelict, but the ground floor of the third is in use as a greengrocers with a pram inventively deployed to support an impromptu market stall.

St John's, Red Lion Square, Holborn, 29 May 1941

Built between 1874-1878 to the design of John Loughborough Pearson, St John's was one of London's finest Victorian churches. In May 1941 it suffered severe damage in an air raid, and even worse through the subsequent stripping of the building for scrap. The ruins were cleared in 1960 for the creation of Procter Street, which obliterated the western end of Red Lion Square.

View from the roof of the adjacent School of Arts & Crafts towards Red Lion Square.

Chapter Eight

WARTIME DEVASTATION

Britain and its Empire was the only power to fight two world wars from beginning to end and emerge on the winning side. The death of over 670 Londoners from aerial bombing in the First World War was a profound psychological shock, demonstrating the acute vulnerability of the capital and its economy to mass air attack. On the eve of the Second World War, the authorities feared 58,000 would die in the first raid alone, but this proved wildly alarmist. London's total war casualties amounted to just under 30,000 killed and over 50,000 seriously injured – shocking enough, but nothing like what had been envisaged.

In 1939 London was the greatest city in the world. By 1945 parts resembled a lunar landscape. The City of London was devastated. Whole districts lay in ruins. Countless historic buildings and places were laid waste. 50,000 houses were destroyed or made irreparable in inner London alone, and over 60,000 in outer London. An additional 290,000 houses suffered serious damage, and a further two million or more slight damage. Stepney lost one-third of its entire housing stock, whilst attacks by V1s and V2s thrust many London suburbs into the front line.

The extent of this destruction can be glimpsed in these photographs. A disproportionate number are City churches, but that is the nature of the archive, which concentrated on recording damage to London's architectural set-pieces.

The bombing provided an unprecedented post-war opportunity to eradicate poverty and squalor and to build a brave new world of modern housing and social amenities – aspirations encapsulated in Sir Patrick Abercrombie's Greater London Plan of 1944. But many streets and districts of fine buildings which could have been refurbished were left to rot, adding even greater momentum to the emerging conservation movement.

Scars of war

Above: Holford Place, Regent's Park, 10 October 1945

Situated in the north-west corner of Regent's Park, Holford House was the largest of the villas designed by Decimus Burton. It was built in 1832 for James Holford, a wealthy merchant and wine importer, with a majestic central portico and apsidal wings. After his death in 1853 it became Regent's Park Baptist College for the training of ministers. Hit by a V1 in 1944, the site was cleared four years later.

Right: New End Square, Hampstead, 12 June 1942

View looking west showing the bombed-out ruins of the square. In the centre foreground is a street shelter. The houses in the background were all carefully repaired after the war, including the Georgian cottages on the extreme right.

Above: Montagu House, 22 Portman Square, 20 June 1941
Montagu House was the salon of the Blue-stocking Club founded by Mrs Elizabeth Montagu, with the object of fostering intellectual debate rather than vacuous social frivolities. Her circle included Horace Walpole, Samuel Johnson and James Boswell. Between 1777-82 she had a mansion built for her to the designs of James Stuart placed diagonally on the north-west corner of the square. One room was decorated entirely with feathers. The house was damaged in May 1941 and, although it could have been saved, it was demolished after the war. The gate piers were dismantled and relocated to Kenwood House.

Right: Montagu House, 22 Portman Square, 9 July 1942
View of the entrance hall and staircase lobby with an Ionic screen in the foreground.

Above: 1-7 St Anne's Court, Soho, 27 February 1949

St Anne's Court links Wardour Street with Dean Street and it still retains a handful of early 18th century houses on its north side. Nos.1-7 on the south side were built in 1735-36 with simple, timber staircases and front and back rooms divided by panelled partitions. By the 1960s this colourful thoroughfare was the haunt of prostitutes and clip joints. The entire terrace was cleared c 1970.

Left: 7 St Anne's Court, Soho, 27 February 1949

View showing the dog-leg corner of the court. Had the terrace survived a few years longer, almost certainly the houses would have been refurbished and converted in a similar fashion to those in Meard Street to the south.

Ruin and loss

Above: St Anne's, Wardour Street, Soho, 5 April 1941
Both Sir Christopher Wren and William Talman were involved in the original design of the church which was consecrated in March 1685, but its peculiar steeple was added by S P Cockerell in 1801-03. Further remodelling took place in the 1830s under Robert Abraham. In 1940 the church was gutted by bombs leaving only the steeple and east end walls which can be seen here. In 1956-57 the site was deconsecrated. Eventually it was redeveloped in the 1980s, retaining the tower and steeple. The novelist Dorothy L Sayers was interred under the tower in 1957.

Right: St James's, Piccadilly, 1941
Built by Wren between 1676-84 to serve the new development of St James's, then being laid out by Henry Jermyn, Earl of St Alban's, on 10 October 1940 the church was damaged severely by high explosives and incendiaries and the Vicarage completely destroyed. After extensive restoration by Sir Albert Richardson, it was rededicated in June 1954 incorporating many original details which survived the bombing, including a Renatus Harris organ from Whitehall Palace and a 17th century reredos by Grinling Gibbons. A new spire designed by Richardson was added in 1968.

Above: Brooke House, Hackney, 4 April 1941

Brooke House was a remarkable mediaeval house with its first recorded orgins in the 1470s. Later it was possessed by Henry Percy, Earl of Northumberland, Thomas Cromwell and various members of the nobility, one of whom, Baron Hunsdon, built the long gallery between 1578-83. From 1759-1940 it was used as a private mental asylum, until October 1940 when it was bit by a high explosive bomb, which destroyed the northern courtyard, seen here, and wrecked the rest of the house. In 1944 it was acquired by the LCC, but after further bomb damage, it was demolished completely in 1954-55; a great loss of a fascinating and historic mediaeval survival.

Right: St Mildred's, Bread Street, City of London, 15 April 1942

St Mildred's was one of Wren's finest and least altered churches. The poet, Shelley, married Mary Wollstonecraft here in 1816. It retained its original pews, pulpit, altar-rails and reredos, until May 1941 when it was destroyed completely in one of London's worst air raids. Only the tower, seen here, was left standing, but subsequently this too was demolished. Virtually nothing remains to mark the site.